Collected Poems

Also by William Jay Smith

POETRY

Poems
Celebration at Dark
Typewriter Birds
The Bead Curtain: Calligrams
Poems 1947–1957
The Tin Can and Other Poems
New & Selected Poems
A Rose for Katherine Anne Porter
Venice in the Fog
Journey to the Dead Sea
The Traveler's Tree: New and Selected Poems
Plain Talk: Epigrams, Epitaphs, Satires, Nonsense, Occasional,
Concrete & Quotidian Poems

(For Children)

Laughing Time: Collected Nonsense
Birds and Beasts
Ho for a Hat!
Boy Blue's Book of Beasts
Puptents and Pebbles: A Nonsense ABC
Typewriter Town
What Did I See?
If I Had a Boat
Mr. Smith and Other Nonsense

TRANSLATIONS

Poems of a Multimillionaire by Valery Larbaud
Selected Writings of Jules Laforgue
Collected Translations: Italian, French, Spanish and Portuguese
(With Leif Sjöberg) *Agadir* by Artur Lundkvist
(With Leif Sjöberg) *Wild Bouquet: Nature Poems* by Harry Martinson
(Editor, with F. D. Reeve) *An Arrow in the Wall: Selected Poetry and Prose*
  by Andrei Voznesensky

Collected Poems

1939–1989

WILLIAM JAY SMITH

CHARLES SCRIBNER'S SONS • *New York*
Collier Macmillan Canada • *Toronto*
Maxwell Macmillan International
New York • *Oxford* • *Singapore* • *Sydney*

ACKNOWLEDGMENTS

Certain of the poems in this collection first appeared in *Poems* (The Banyan Press), 1947; *Celebration at Dark* (Farrar, Straus & Young), 1950; *Poems 1947–1957* (Atlantic-Little, Brown), 1957; *The Tin Can and Other Poems* (Seymour Lawrence-Delacorte), 1966; *New and Selected Poems* (Seymour Lawrence-Delacorte), 1970; *Venice in the Fog* (Unicorn Press), 1975; *Journey to the Dead Sea* (Abattoir), 1979; *The Traveler's Tree: New and Selected Poems* (Persea Books), 1980; *Laughing Time: Nonsense Poems* (Seymour Lawrence-Delacorte), 1980; and in the following magazines: *The Beloit Poetry Journal, The Formalist, The New Criterion, Poetry, The New Republic, The New Yorker, The Southern Review.*

Charles Scribner's Sons
Macmillan Publishing Company
866 Third Avenue, New York, NY 10022

Collier Macmillan Canada, Inc.
1200 Eglinton Avenue, Suite 200
Don Mills, Ontario M3C 3N1

Library of Congress Cataloging-in-Publication Data
Smith, William Jay, 1918–
[Poems]
Collected poems : 1939–1989 / William Jay Smith.
p.   cm.
ISBN 0-684-19167-9
I. Title.
PS3537.M8693A17   1990
811'.54—dc20   90-40760   CIP

Macmillan books are available at special discounts for bulk purchases for sales promotions, premiums, fund-raising, or educational use.
For details, contact:

Special Sales Director
Macmillan Publishing Company
866 Third Avenue
New York, NY 10022

Designed by Paolo Pepe

10 9 8 7 6 5 4 3 2 1

Printed in the United States of America

To
Sonja

Contents

I have arranged the poems in this collection by section, in approximate chronological order. The poems in each section, however, although written within the time indicated, do not appear chronologically. A single date on a section is the date of book publication.

I have restored a few poems that were published many years after they were written to the time of their original composition. "Quail in Autumn," not published until the sixties, was actually one of my earliest poems, and it appears here in the opening section where it belongs. "Pidgin Pinch," also first published in the sixties, was drafted during World War II and appears now with the War Poems. A number of the latter are collected here for the first time.

My revisions of the early poems have been minor. I have cut a stanza and changed a few lines here and there but have done no extensive rewriting. I have included none of my translations from various languages because they have been, or are being, collected elsewhere. My children's poems, also collected elsewhere, are represented by only a few examples which have appeared previously in my adult collections. I have likewise included only a small selection of my light and occasional verse since most of it is also being published separately.

I am grateful to Dana Gioia and Henry Taylor for the valuable assistance they have given me in assembling this collection.

W. J. S.

QUAIL IN AUTUMN

(1939–1940)

Quail in Autumn

Autumn has turned the dark trees toward the hill;
The wind has ceased; the air is white and chill.
Red leaves no longer dance against your foot,
The branch reverts to tree, the tree to root.

And now in this bare place your step will find
A twig that snaps flintlike against the mind;
Then thundering above your giddy head,
Small quail dart up, through shafting sunlight fled.

Like brightness buried by one's sullen mood
The quail rise startled from the threadbare wood;
A voice, a step, a swift sun-thrust of feather
And earth and air come properly together.

The Young Lovers

These two went with cautious smile,
Edged with hope, a touch of fear,
Over a windy, whirling mile
Into a quiet sphere.

There to an island shaped with green
Corners descending to a shell
Holding a bay where silence fell
On reef and tree.

I saw them treading morning light
That seeped from sand, from palm
And bush, again at night—
Two shadows huge and calm

Stretched before the wave; I heard
Their cry like the cry of children who, in play,
Pursue a darting sky-blue bird
And find their bird at the end of day.

He Will Not Hear

He will not see the leaf-green sky
Spread high above him, white with cloud anemone;
He will not follow high

Into the trees across the hills
The sharply throbbing thigh of wind, nor watch
For blood the poppy spills.

He will not meet the huge furred
Side of darkness, impelled
Into a word.

The singer's voice will never gain
His ear; his flesh will be inviolable
Beneath the caterpillar softness of the rain.

He will not hear; he will not walk in wonder
Through the seasons, torn
By their transparent thunder.

DARK VALENTINE
War Poems

(1940–1945)

The Vision

He stood above you and the mountain flamed;
And all the fish beneath you swam like spears.
The lion roared, which once the dove had tamed;
And the eagle perched on his eye.

The planets kept their certain, savage courses;
The moon from high
Released the waves like twenty thousand horses
Whose teeth were shears.

O mourn for the world as I mourn this morning
In a cloak that is made of Job's-tears.

The Massacre of the Innocents

Because I believe in the community of little children,
Because I have suffered such little children to be slain;
I have gazed upon the sunlight, dazed, bewildered,
As is a child by nothing more than rain.

Not until I can no longer climb,
Until my life becomes the tallest tree,
And every limb of it a limb of shame,
Shall I look out in time, in time to see

Again those who were so small they could but die,
Who had only their vast innocence to give,
That I may tell them, pointing down the sky,
How beautiful it might have been to live.

Au Tombeau du Maréchal Pet-de-Nain

Travelers, pause—and lift your caps.
Bow your heads in the sun.
If your ears are good, you can hear perhaps
taps at Carcassonne.

He mounted upon his milk-white steed
and led his people down the drain
with the Order of the Centipede
on a shield of cellophane.

His people cherished ancient roots,
their faith was sorely shaken:
he rode to the Spa and slicked his boots,
and had his picture taken.

His people asked him what to do.
He said: "Lay down your gun
and to the Centipede be true."
—He had stopped them at Verdun.

Travelers, pause—and lift your caps.
Bow your heads in the sun.
If your ears are good, you can hear perhaps
taps at Carcassonne.

Convoy

The ships are fitted, and the convoy sails;
our course is toward the east and to the sun.
Antennae turn, our only contact whales;
we seek the Jonah who inhabits one.
Airborne the continents above us meet,
below lie cities which we lean to hear.
The sea unwinds like the ends of Easy Street,
where no one goes straight but all will come out in the clear.

Not like the islander with outrigged craft,
nor Jack who journeyed high upon the bean,
have we for long days roamed the decks and laughed
aboard these liberties! I do not mean
we have been comfortable, nor, for that matter, clean.
Ask the man struck dead by the lifeboat somewhere aft.

3 for 25

Downing his drink to toasts of cut-rate jokes,
The sailor on the 10-day leave, the Machinist's Mate
2nd, squares his tousled halo for the folks,
And looks into the camera as at fate.
There where the painted palm tree's tonic sway
Recedes, authentic as a tourist folder,
Vast bridges spanning a blue bay,
As real as horseshoes float back from his shoulder.

10 days are not enough; but the Machinist's Mate
2nd leaves of his life this urgent pose,
These meerschaum fingers, eyes like dominoes:
And this one act, like all his holiday,
Is right only if he remains in black and white
When camera clicks with quick, conclusive fact.

Poem near Pearl Harbor

(1942)

—The ladies who gather beneath the hau tree
play bridge by flashlight near the sea.—

Darkness falls; the breakers break.
Over the breakers Diamond Head
exhibits like a wedding cake
its crest of gingerbread.

The beacons on the orange sands
thrust their knives in indigo;
the cake will not crumble in the bridegroom's hands—
he left here long ago.

—The ladies with flashlight under the tree
tap the pineapple in their tea.—

Their smile is set in nickelplate
where late beneath the twisted stacks
an Oklahoman Pharmacist's Mate
stowed the blood-encrusted blacks.

Darkness falls; the tension mounts.
Their eyelids blue as the skin of grapes,
they grip their shabby honor counts
of tinsel-throated jackanapes.

Darkness falls; the breakers break.
Over the breakers Diamond Head
with the shrouded beaks of mynah birds
salutes the dying and the dead.

Hotel Continental

O I feel like the kinks in the paws of the Sphinx!
  O I've got those combustible keys!
On goes the phone with a tone all its own:
  P—lease! P—lease! P—lease!

The room is a yawn. The room is war.
  On the velvet gallop the dice.
Man O'Man, one foot on the bar-
  rail, sways with sacrifice.

Where once the star-spangled ocean broke,
  Now Caesar's cymbals clash;
We speak the French our fathers spoke
  And dance the *java vache*.

Laugh, my pigeon, laugh. Your car is ready.
  Laugh. Your chauffeur waits without the door.
His hands are clean, his eye is clear and steady.
  He drives a Quisling '44.

Laugh, my pigeon, laugh. Lift up the lever.
  Our souls are Chinamen along the wall.
They live as long as we (which is forever);
  They rise as pure as laughter when we fall.

O I feel like the kinks in the paws of the Sphinx!
  O I've got those negotiable knees!
On goes the phone with a tone all its own:
  P—lease! P—lease! P—lease!

Dark Valentine

An Apollonian invocation in wartime

This daylit doll, this dim divinity,
who wipes his chin upon his frothy cuff,
and sits beside you there and combs his curls,
as suspect as a Romanoff;

who with the inward ease of the ventriloquist
makes his insolence so crystalline,
fumbling the bomber-bracelet on his wrist
to the boogie-woogie of the radar screen:

Is this the Deity of your Devotions,
Lamb of all your Litanies?
Is this the Olifant of all the Oceans,
the Salamander of some Seven Seas?

Is it he who clicked his heels and roundly laughed
and sent your fortress whirling past the sun,
gave you Christ as a fourth upon the raft,
and added a day at each meridian?

Is it he who rose above the ruined Rhine,
the Ganymede and Gremlin of your guilt,
fled among fiddles, one dark valentine
stuffed in the laurel at his hilt?

With the force of the brute and the lilt of the little lark,
so precious, so baroque, almost archaic,
see how he drives the dolphin down the dark
into the amber sunlight like mosaic.

Is it for him the brightest suns have set?
Is it for him the proudest cities burn?
Still in our minds his jewels pirouette,
still in our hearts his cold propellers turn.

Is this the Deity of your Devotions,
Lamb of all your Litanies?
Is this the Olifant of all the Oceans,
the Salamander of some Seven Seas?

                    *   *   *

Advance, advance and be recognized!
speaks the God of Love from the golden limb.
And we advance. Is Love disguised?
He is. As you imagined him.

Elegy

O flots abracadabrantesques,
Prenez mon coeur qu'il soit lavé.

—Arthur Rimbaud

Look to the heavens, Heliotrope.
Follow the sun. Sun, shine!
The streets are numbered, shelled and soft:
Eleventh, Olive, Chestnut, Pine.

Mannikins puff pale cigarettes,
Club girls clench calypso-colas;
From verdant rooftops yeomanettes
Succinctly sigh: *Sobre las olas:*

You shipped him off address unknown
You shipped him far beyond Endurance
I cannot reach him on the phone
He left me all his life insurance.

Look to the heavens, Heliotrope.
Follow the sun. Sun, shine!
The streets are numbered, shelled and soft:
Eleventh, Olive, Chestnut, Pine.

Epithalamium in Olive Drab

O orange were her underclothes,
  her nails were hothouse pink,
when Rosalind, in jungle rose,
  was wed in a roller rink.

        The bells ring true: True-blue True-blue.
          She was cheery; he was chipper.
        They did not fly to Ho - no - lu - lu
          in the cabin of a clipper.

With the frontal lobe of Jackie Cooper
  and the soul of General Grant,
Paul is now a paratrooper
  and Roz rivets in a plant.

        The bells ring true: True-blue True-blue.
          She was cheery; he was chipper.
        They did not fly to Ho - no - lu - lu
          in the cabin of a clipper.

They lie elate from six to eight
  at the Mars Moontide Motel.
Of the union I celebrate
  more I may not tell.

        The bells ring true: True-blue True-blue.
          She was cheery; he was chipper.
        They did not fly to Ho - no - lu - lu
          in the cabin of a clipper.

Barber, Wartime

Seaman First Class, name of Cartocelli,
Clipper-quick, adept at dialects,
Trigger finger poised above the belly,
Trims the dormant intellects.

Off there, the long white razor of the reef
Slashes lather through the slender trees;
A mynah bird berates a breadfruit leaf,
Light trails, hairy round one's knees.

Off there, in faded blue the men go walking,
There, grim and gray, a dusty lorry comes;
Evening; bugles, and the blur of talking;
And the darker sound of drums.

What are life and death to Cartocelli,
Who shears the domes his dimming glass reflects?
Night falls; men die—to him details are silly,
And trim, the dormant intellects.

Pidgin Pinch

Joe, you Big Shot! You Big Man!
You Government Issue! You Marshall Plan!

Joe, you got plenty Spearmint Gum?
I change you Money, you gimme Some!

Joe, you want Shoe-Shine, Cheap Souvenir?
My Sister overhaul you Landing Gear?

Joe, you Queer Kid? Fix-you Me?
Dig-Dig? Buzz-Buzz? Reefer? Tea?

Joe, I find you Belly Dance,
Trip Around the World—Fifty Cents!

Joe, you got Cigarette? Joe, you got Match?
Joe, you got Candy? You Sum-Bitch,

You think I Crazy? I waste my Time?
I give you *Trouble?* Gimme a *Dime!*

Movies for the Troops

I

In Hollywood the pale white stars
Slump (drunk and jeweled) in Milk Bars,
Or tour the palm-lined avenues
In gently rocking open cars.

II

The burly boys off to the wars
To die (with mention in the news)
Accept these images that fuse,
And clap their hands, and thank their stars.

Columbus Circle Swing

Old Mr. Christopher sailed an egg
to prove that it was round
while the man at the keg with the wooden leg
stood his ground.

Brothers Wright, perfecting flight,
let the rabbit out of the hat:
Now overhead the quadruped
disputes his habitat.

O where shall we go when it rains all the day,
and what shall we do when it's over:
will the day be as bright when it dawns at Calais
as it was after dark at Dover?

Bombers roar off overhead,
turn down your shaded lamps.
The cities burn, a Christmas red,
smoke rises from the camps.

The world's an egg, ah, through and through.
It was decided for us.
You can always change a line or two;
you cannot change the chorus.

O where shall we go when it rains all the day,
and what shall we do when it's over:
will the day be as bright when it dawns at Calais
as it was after dark at Dover?

Villanelle

You rise to walk yet when you fly you sit;
The young are not so young as the old are old:
People with hair are always combing it.

The mountain now can come to Mahomet,
An offering on wings of beaten gold:
You rise to walk yet when you fly you sit.

Malherbe, whose rhetoric obscured his wit,
Read poems to his cook when dolphins bowled:
People with hair are always combing it.

This pig, the World, is roasted on a spit;
That pig today were better pigeonholed:
You rise to walk yet when you fly you sit.

We comb the country for the shoes that fit;
The mushroom grows where now the wings unfold:
People with hair are always combing it.

The laurel has been cut, the flares are lit;
The people wait, the pilot's hands are cold:
You rise to walk yet when you fly you sit;
People with hair are always combing it.

LOOKING-GLASS WORLD

(1940–1950)

The Barber

The barber who arrives to cut my hair
Looks at his implements, and then at me.
The world is a looking glass in which I see
A toadstool in the shape of a barber chair.

The years are asleep. A fly crawls on the edge
Of a broken cup, and a fan in the corner whines.
The barber's hands move over me like vines
In a dream as long as hair can ever grow.

Reflection

As from a rainbow, the canoe
Is launched on a lagoon
Below the house.

Under bright boughs,
Lizard-blue, the water
Licks the gray stone,

And the trades blow calm.
Upon my wall, the shadow of a giant palm
Branch bends, a claw, a hand,

Like all reality in reflection
Caught, out of time, beyond waves' hum,
And wind's delirium.

Rage, wild water. For the world
Rides my eye, as evermore
The canoe its element.

Academic Procession

Conversant with a day no longer ours,
the cool fact, the deed done,
they walk now in sunlight through spring flowers
in unison.

Ah, they walk down the choral paths in spring,
and theirs is the world to bear;
like old incensers lilacs fling
fragrance down the air.

Through many centuries of spring they come,
and time is left for clocks
to tell, or watches soft as the bee's hum
in their dark frocks.

Now from the clean, funereal wood
all earthly creatures humbly greet
the festive father with the checkered hood
and the chaste pleat.

The cherub smiles, and then turns back,
angels lay aside their harps;
this day's for earth's own guardians who but lack
the central corpse.

A Note on the Vanity Dresser

The yes-man in the mirror now says no,
No longer will I answer you with lies.
The light descends like snow, so when the snow-
man melts, you will know him by his eyes.

The yes-man in the mirror now says no.
Says no. No double negative of pity
Will save you now from what I know you know:
These are your eyes, the cinders of your city.

The Farm

Old MacDonald had a farm
  A long time ago
Before we had a School of Charm
  With an ee - i ee - i - o.

And on that farm he had a tire
  Hung from a branch as a swing,
An O that held a world entire,
  Encircling everything:

We gazed through the tire at a house on a hill,
  At a house in a tall oak tree,
At a bright blue jay with a busy bill
  And a song like a door key.

We gazed on a hill, a cold white star,
  May apple and wild rose,
On fireflies trapped in a Mason jar,
  And on corn in tall, neat rows.

We saw through the tire the little Ford cars
  That into their graveyard go;
They go to bed with our movie stars,
  Rin-Tin-Tin, Clara Bow.

We saw, as they turned, the barber poles,
  The band that marched on the green,
The bittersweet paths and the dark sinkholes
  Where Indian lean-tos lean.

We followed the river that overflowed
   Its broad mud-flats in spring
And lifted farmhouses off the dirt road
   Like the toys of a mad brown king.

Old MacDonald had a farm:
   Wind and rain and snow
Never do the slightest harm—
   With an ee - i ee - i - o.

Old Men on the Bench

How faultless fall their shadows on the faulted rocks
  Like knotted vines upon wine-colored pools.
Old men should be deprived of calendars and clocks.
  Eternity is after April Fools.

The Earth is invaded by men from the World of Now;
  It has no pinnacle they cannot reach.
The opulent orange darkens on the bough,
  Light from that sun-swept garden peels like a peach.

The lines have now been manned on all dry docks,
  The dolphin are unwound as if from spools.
Old men should be deprived of calendars and clocks,
  Of keys and locks; of rulers, and of rules.

A Locket for Emily Dickinson

She walked into the church in early spring,
  Upon her father's arm a pretty picture . . .
—And in her dream she took a lover's ring,
  An emblem of delight and of conjecture.

Her life entire was like a letter home,
  A letter which no other woman wrote.
Read it with love: the lover bears no name;
  Her lineage lies golden on her throat.

Abruptly All the Palm Trees

Abruptly all the palm trees rose like parasols,
and sunlight danced, and green to greenness gave.
Birds flew forth and cast like waterfalls
shadow upon shade.

Where the crab with its linoleum colors crawls,
and coral combs the crystal-caverned sea,
we stood, our blood as bright and fringed as shawls
before the delicate expanding leaf.

Abruptly all the palm trees rose like parasols,
and green was the green that green to greenness gave.
Dimension crumbled, Time laid down its walls;
and all the world went wading toward the wave.

At the Terminal

Time's perched upon the wrist in fond farewell
Intent as lions filmed on cameos.
Along the sultry hallways into hell,
The doors revolve, revolve; and do not close.
The attendant in the darkening anteroom
Signs the ransom note with one sweep of his plume.

Time feeds upon the wrist: his glass is low,
Abundant are the sands which nurture him.
The dark vine lies in place like an ancient bow;
Thoughts, cold swans, on sable waters swim:
While Memory, the Peacock, has unfurled
More spots than there are capitals in the world.

Time's perched upon the wrist, and is forever,
Like the world which is the work of one whole week.
At the delta of my fingers, O no river
Melts the ice on that subversive peak.
Green's the signal, Love, where now you go
As there the Peacock moves upon the snow.

CELEBRATION AT DARK

(1950)

Chrysanthemums

I had, here in the room before you came,
A dark delight announcing as with drums
Your coming, and the closing of the door,
Upon a tabletop, obese and tame,
These lion-headed flowers,
Four chrysanthemums.

A painter would have loved them, and been glad
To have them within reach: to see
Is mad, and madness teaches
Nothing if not love.
Great kings lay murdered in the flower beds:
I had, upon a table in this room,
Their four crowned heads.

In life we are often lonely, wanting death,
A kind of love not quite
Like this, a somnolence of light,
A glory which is native to the sun,
A poem in the landscape brooded on.

Dark springs, how dark;
And from the world's four corners, flowers
Like the heads of shaven Danes,
Huge and listless lions' manes,
Look down upon us where we lie
In darkness now, and overpowered die
Of love, of love.

The Peacock of Java

I thought of the mariners of Solomon,
Who, on one of their long voyages, came
   On that rare bird, the Peacock
   Of Java, which brings, even
To the tree of heaven, heaven.

How struggling upward through the dark
   Lianas, they beheld the tree,
   And in the tree, the fan
That would become a king's embroidery.

How they turned and on the quiet
   Water then set sail
   For home, the peacock's tail
Committed to the legends of the sea.

Orpheus

Orpheus with music charms the birds
And animals, the fish, the falling waves,
The stars that might be starfish overhead,
And dragons in their oriental caves.
By men who suffer he is always heard,
And speaks of life, and death which darkness brings,
Of roads that wind like sorrow through the trees,
Of forests, and of hills like sleeping kings.

Let us prepare; the god of music comes.
He will have laurel, and a fountain playing,
Moon-men ready at the kettledrums,
Fire-tipped lances, moon-white horses neighing,
Earth awaking from her tragic sleep,
The cool, ecstatic earth. O hear, O hear.

The Girl in Glass

"You've stood there long enough," I said,
"Combing your hair. The pyramids
Are built; the traveler back
From ruined Thebes, Luxor, Karnak,
Has told the tale." You stopped.
And then, with fingers weaving,
Both white hands
Infiltrating copper strands
Of hair, began again.

Began, and then the delta sands
Ran out; you were a star-
Lit bloom, a water flower
Opening hour after hour
As I lay watching you in bed,
And the lamp burned low, and coral-red.

A mermaid in a fable wanted
To become a woman, and was nailed
With diamonds to my wall;
So Love, beside a waterfall,
Broke off a branch of berries from a tree,
And planted it at midnight
In the sea.

"You've stood there long enough."

Persian Miniature

Ah, all the sands of the earth lead unto heaven.
I have seen them rise on the wind, a golden thread,
The sands of the earth which enter the eye of heaven,
Over the graves, the poor, white bones of the dead.
Over the buckling ice, the swollen rivers,
Over the ravened plains, and the dry creek-beds,
The sands are moving. I have seen them move,
And where the pines are bent, the orient
Grain awaits the passage of the wind.
Higher still the laden camels thread
Their way beyond the mountains, and the clouds
Are whiter than the ivory they bear
For Death's black eunuchs. Gold, silk, furs
Cut the blood-red morning. All is vain.
I have watched the caravans through the needle's eye
As they turn, on the threshing floor, the bones of the dead,
And green as a grasshopper's leg is the evening sky.

Morning at Arnhem

I

From the cassowary's beak come streaks of light,
Morning, and possibility.
In the countries of the north
Ice breaks, and breaking, blossoms forth
With possibility; and day abounds
In light and color, color, sounds.

II

In Holland there are tulips on the table,
A wind from the north on the gray stones
That breaks the heart, and sits upon the shoulder,
And turns the mill, the pine cones.

Waking below the level of the sea,
You wake in peace; the gardens look
Like roofs of palaces beneath the water,
And into the sea the land hooks.

In Holland there are tulips on the table,
A wind from the north on the gray stones
That breaks the heart, and turns, with the mill at cockrow,
Over the quiet dead, the pine cones.

III

From the cassowary's beak come streaks of light;
A wrought-iron angel mounts a weather vane; you might
Be anywhere in Europe now that night
Is over, and you see that life begins like this
In tragedy: in light that is entangled in the leaves,
And morning shaken from an angel's sleeves;
And you can turn to face the mouth
Of the great black lion of heaven,
The terrible, beautiful south.

The Park in Milan

The animals we have seen, all marvelous creatures,
The lion king, the pygmy antelope,
The zebra like a convict cutting corners,
Birds in cages, orioles and doves,
The sacred ibis with a beak like a gravy dish,
Tropical fish weaving a Persian carpet
For the dancing feet of sunlight, marvelous creatures,
Theirs is the kingdom of love.

       Love we have brought them
On a summer day, weary from walking;
Like children who cool their faces on piano keys,
We turn to the quiet park, the good, green trees,
And a wealth of animal being runs in our minds like music.

Like music all the miracles of being,
The flash and fire of sunlight and of sound,
The elephant in cage of muted thunder,
Zebras on the shaken, shaded ground.

Turning from them now like children turning,
We watch the city open like a wound,
With gutted church and bombed and broken buildings,
Girders like black bones that lace the void,
All we build through love through hate destroyed,
The world an aged animal that heaves and cries
Under the trees, the gay, green trees of summer.

Music fades; the streets are black with flies.

The Closing of the Rodeo

The lariat snaps, the cowboy rolls
   His pack, and mounts and rides away.
Back to the land the cowboy goes.

Plumes of smoke from the factory sway
   In the setting sun. The curtain falls,
A train in the darkness pulls away.

Good-bye, says the rain on the iron roofs.
   Good-bye, say the barber poles.
Dark drum the vanishing horses' hooves.

The Inhabitants of Atlantis

In an aquarium above the bar, the fish,
   In their nefarious necktie colors,
   Ancestral, swim.

The arms of the drinkers move in reflection
   Like the booms of freighters loading
   In the semidarkness

Their golden cargo: now the room's
   A sea of light where all
   Must drown, the fish

Go down like divers to the rock; the sailors
   Drown the green-back darting
   Dolphin in their eyes:

While in the dim blue distance clangs a bell
   Which echoes through the flooded room,
   And underwater dies.

Summertime

Spotted leopards stroll the avenue;
The caterpillars come and they are green,
Yukon yellow, chocolate, basement blue.

A Sunday painter would enjoy the view,
The morning glories heavy on the strings,
The quiet converse of the avenue.

Stealthy jungle shadows come and go;
Roosters flail the dust, and meadows run
Beyond the reach of light serene and slow.

Like cargoes riverboats might jettison,
White clouds collect upon the country air
Or drop below the rooftops one by one.

The sun, old spot, sits gaudy in the wings,
And cocks his head, and combs his flaming hair:
Spotted leopards stroll the avenue.

Ballad from Bedlam

Let Huldah bless with the silkworm—the ornaments of the proud
are from the bowells of their Betters.

—Christopher Smart

The firefly corresponds in urgent letters;
He is repaid in the notes of the nightingale.
The gullet of the shark rides out the gale:
Our ornament derives from the bowels of our betters.

My grandfather, Billy Smith, had an Irish setter's
Piercing eye, and a temper quicker than quail.
Faith was the name of his wife; she was hard as a nail:
Our ornament derives from the bowels of our betters.

Undertakers are the real go-getters;
Give me the Glory Road, the Oregon Trail,
A worm to clothe the Proud, a peak to scale:
Our ornament derives from the bowels of our betters.

God bless the hermit crab, the Veter-
An of Foreign Wars, the intestine of the whale,
The old man's rattle, and the infant's wail:
Our ornament derives from the bowels of our betters.

Cupidon

"To love is to give," said the crooked old man.
  "To love is to be poor."
And he led me up his accordion stair,
  And closed his iron door.

"To love is to give." His words like wire
  Dragged the ocean floor.
"Throw ten of your blankets on the fire,
  Then throw ten thousand more."

His room was the prayer on the head of a pin.
  As clean as a diamond cut
Was the iron door which opened in
  And would not open out.

"To love is to give, to give, to give.
  Give more and more and more."
And the wind crept up his accordion stair,
  And under his iron door.

The Diving Bell

Like one endangered in a diving bell
I move submerged, alone in the open sea.
Alive in love, I move in a lonely bell,
Driven alone into the open sea.

Immortal is the murderer who works my lines,
And all this air of heaven to no good;
Works me in loops, loops me in liquid vine
And takes me to his tangled water-wood.

Lost is the voice of the dark in dark dissolving,
Lost in the somnolent surf, the summer-swell.
I move in this world in such sonorous weather
On ocean bed I break from broken bell.

On Parting

Time that is recorded is not now,
Now when the train is leaving, and the clock
Is hooded in the distance, when the heart cries: How
Can you be leaving, for there is no time?

Some delight in the journey, in the crossing
Of accepted boundaries; you go
Knowing you love what's left, yourself, your loss
Of—
    Knowing the wheels will say, You do not know.

Rain is falling, and there is no rest.
Where are there tears enough to drown the sun?
Love also dies; the dead have loved you best:
Look for them there in the dark where the rails run.

Of Islands

Of all the islands sailing down the west,
Of islands sailing north and south and east,
It is not islands you remember best—
Or better, have forgotten least.

It is not land, the quick, sure touch of trees,
Not all the lusty continent which sense reveals,
Which floats upon the mind immense with ease,
And steals away as quick as darkness steals.

It is not islands. It is less than islands,
Land still land until at once you see
You have come upon a calm, enclosed lagoon
And earth in its entirety:

And since it is an interim of sea and air,
Even as islands ultimately are,
And the waves are clouds which crawl back up the sky
To overtake a star:

Then even if the land is land no man can mend,
Which salt nor sand nor star can clean,
This is the island which our lives defend,
Where life must end, and death put forth its green.

Nukuhiva

Nukuhiva, the scene of Melville's Typee, *is one of the Marquesas Islands.*
The islanders whom Melville describes are now almost extinct.

For Stephen Spender

I

It was in time of war, and yet no war,
No sound of war, and scarce the memory of one
So terrible that none forget, troubled
Our passage, the ship's dark keel breaking
The phosphorescent water, foam riding the halyards.
Far, far, far from home, the sailor busy with the day's routine,
We came one morning where the mountains rose
Upon a semicircular and emerald bay,
And a few birds circled like a flaw,
To the beautiful island of Nukuhiva.

Here Melville came, pursuing and pursued,
An angry spirit in a lasting rage,
Came tracked by time and all its skeletal
Transactions, the decay of empires, tracked
By life and death, and worlds of lies,
To Nukuhiva, and the whaleback bay,
An animal that listens with its eyes.

Seaweed trailed from scupper-hole, and folded sail,
The whaler rode the water, and the sailor's gaze
Went out to greet the islanders, the great
Canoes tilting with stalwart oarsmen, and the girls
As gold as morning diving from the surf,
The scent of oil and flowers.

II

The ship's boat swung
From the davits, then the wildcat purr of motors broke
The circling silence, and the jumbled rocks ashore
Came nearer, steady, up, the whip and lash of waves.

This was a place that memory corrupts,
A tumbling house half-seen through green and mottled
Foliage. The Frenchman talked of Paris and of youth,
Of Suez and Arabia and the East,
While the furious sunlight beat upon the rocks,
And words crept out like lizards on the leaves—
Bird-song, wind-song, sun.

The horses waited, cropping the dry brown grass
By the open gate, the crumbling wall; we swung
Into the saddle, sunlight flecking the hooves.

What was the island then? And who will say,
The wind, the sun, the moon? So much is buried there
In what was scarce a century ago
The center of a commerce and a colony,
Amalgam of Soho and a Yukon town,
Where drunken planter strode, and trader dipped,
And the bishop like a fat persimmon sat
Under the green palmetto in the afternoon.

III

Up, up, up, we rode through trees and tangled vines,
Struggling as one struggles in a dream
Across a moving mass of melting snow,
Words fail, the trail is lost among the trees.
Up the temple steps, the chipped, black stone
Breaking the clumsy branches, horses' froth
Smelling of papaya and mango.

Winding and unwinding like a leash,
We came to the burial platforms, the plateau,
And heard the water crashing through the vines,
And heard behind us, upward from the bay:
Revenez, revenez! On avait des copains!
Always in a language that was never mine.

Nukuhiva, Hivaoa, Raiatea,
The islands and the names are poetry,
And they are spoken by the voices of the drowning,
By the voices of the men who are remembered
By the cold, white, lonely presence of the sea.

IV

Whatever we had come for lay behind,
And what we sought lay still ahead.
As we approached the beach, the west was red;
The pom-poms of the sailors danced upon the waves
Like poppies on the distant fields of Brittany
Across the semicircular and horseshoe bay,
And all the wailing places of the dead.

The Lady in Orange County

Beautiful lady, loops of country road
In the County of Orange took me where,
Oh, my olive-backed sunbird, you stood
Greeting the bathers.

There was a freshness in your glance,
A freshness which the bamboo has perhaps
In its cool segments in the jungle shade.

The mountains knelt; cicadas made
Oriental music and you danced
Over the swaying grasses.

In autumn now returning to the shore,
I do not find the bathers; they have gone
To pick persimmons in the woods.

Beyond the holly branches where the clouds
Are touched with silver, and a bird
Dips in blood a red quill,

High on a balcony you stand,
And hear the galloping horsemen come
Out of the hollow over the hill.

Galileo Galilei

Comes to knock and knock again
At a small secluded doorway
In the ordinary brain.

Into light the world is turning,
And the clocks are set for six;
And the chimney pots are smoking,
And the golden candlesticks.

Apple trees are bent and breaking,
And the heat is not the sun's;
And the Minotaur is waking,
And the streets are cattle runs.

Galileo Galilei,
In a flowing, scarlet robe,
While the stars go down the river
With the turning, turning globe,

Kneels before a black Madonna
And the angels cluster round
With grave, uplifted faces
Which reflect the shaken ground

And the orchard which is burning,
And the hills which take the light;
And the candles which have melted
On the altars of the night.

Galileo Galilei
Comes to knock and knock again
At a small secluded doorway
In the ordinary brain.

Miserere

The lights have gone out in the School for the Blind,
   And all the shades are drawn.
   Sisters of Mercy move over the lawn.

Sisters of Mercy move into the mind
   With steps that are swifter than any;
   Light on each pupil is perched like a penny.

The lights have gone out in the School for the Blind;
   The flare on the runway dies,
   And the murderer waits with dancing eyes.

The murderer waits in the quiet mind,
   While Night, a Negress nun,
   A Sister of Mercy, sweeps over the sun.

The Wooing Lady

Once upon the earth at the midnight hour,
When all the bells are ringing in the wood,
A lady lies alone in a palace tower,
And yet must woo, and yet must still be wooed.

She glides upon the stair, a bird on water,
In costly sable clad, in seven sins,
To lie beside her knight, a king's white daughter,
A scullery maid beneath the marten skins.

The stars are out, and all the torches lit.
Below the window is an orange tree,
Catching the light and then returning it,
A juggler in an antique tapestry.

Horses gallop away; the boughs are shaken
So gently it can hardly be believed.
And over all the world the birds awaken
As he awakens, beautifully deceived.

On the Islands Which Are Solomon's

On the islands which are Solomon's I sometimes see
A swift, black bird which on wild pepper feeds;
And having reached a mild satiety,
Casts off its song like a merry widow's weeds.

Rich in wisdom from the shady bed of time
The islands rise, and to our world belong.
The hills are hot, the shores are cool with lime:
Hop to my hand, dark beauty, stripped of song.

Vincent van Gogh

Walking at night in a hat fitted with twelve candles,
The painter came to the edge of a field, and a barbed wire
Fence, and that was all.
The corn was ablaze, and the sky caught fire.

The stars were extinguished; the painter died,
Blood from his hand running into the flower beds.
Here is the cornfield, swirling ear, and all;
And in the foreground, nervously applied,
An intricate maze of thin-sown poppyheads.

Dark, Dark, Dark

Time after time after time comes El Tiempo,
Galloping on upon the prairie, time
After time after time after time at a terrible tempo,
Galloping on to the end, he ends in time.

Below the pockmarked hills, the ravaged mountains,
He rides the plain, and fords the flashing stream;
While clouds of smoke engulf the crackling branches,
And dark descends on village, field, and stream.

The stars go up like flares from the tarpaper roofs,
And their jagged light is drunk by the autumn leaves;
While the ancient earth absorbs the pounding hooves,
The wind removes the leaves, the burning leaves.

O Love, O Love, These Oceans Vast

He who has felt on his dark bed
  The pressure of the tides
Finds sunlight ebbing round his head,
  Morning on all sides.

Like all heaven the hound will eat from his hand,
  And the wave like a newborn foal;
Manes engulfing a green island,
  Lions court his soul.

Lions that walk the yellow sand
  On the blood of morning fed;
And he who wakes finds light, his land;
  Darkness, fleeing, fled.

Elegy

For Bateman Edwards, d. 1 Sept. 1947

I stood between two mirrors when you died,
Two mirrors in a dimly lighted hall,
Identical in all respects.
Two mirrors face to face reflecting endlessly
Reflection's end.
The wind that had been blowing died away,
Or in the distance seemed about to die.
I stood between two mirrors in the hall.

Outside, the wheels had cut the gravel, and the sun-
Flower nodded to the sun; the air was still.
The deer that browsed upon a distant hillside
Lifted his antlers like a coral tree
Forgotten in midsummer undersea.
And from the delicate dark bridges which the spider
Spun from branch to branch,
In desolation hung
One leaf, announcing autumn to the world.

The world that evening was a world of mirrors
Where two great dragons from opposing caves,
Mirror their eyes and mirror all the scales
Of their long bodies and their giant tails,
Emerged. And all that had seemed human was confined
In terror in the limits of the mind,
And coiled, uncoiled within my memory.

In your sudden dying you became the night
Which I must add to darkness now
To make the morning bright,
To have day break, and daybreak
Melt the mirrors. But I know
You cannot hear me now although
I say, dear friend, good morning and good night.

Italian Song

Bigger than belladonna makes the eyes
(And it's a mark of beauty not to see),
The heart must swell, tell fortune how time flies,
Tell time to stop, and not to be to be.

It is a mark of beauty to be seen,
Belladonna, and your eyes are black
As Gold Coast Negroes on the bowling green,
Or cinders from a locomotive stack.

Olives on bright branches ripening
Are not to be compared with eyes like that;
If eyes that black are black as anything,
It is a bowler in a stovepipe hat.

It is an evening on the Russian Steppes
When snow is falling and a black hawk flies
As high as Everest against the moon,
Bigger than belladonna makes the eyes.

Evening at Grandpoint

Who under a stone bridge in the dark
Has seen?—We saw there, remember, wait,
The wind falls, wait, the street
Is empty now the leaves, the leaves
Are flocking to your feet—

Two swans, their floating, fluted necks
Down under feathers' whiteness,
Snow-plumed birds, awake?—No,
Not awake, two birds there deep
Down under thunder rocking,
Cradled, swans asleep.

Tell me, will you?—Well I know
How deep the swirling waters go
Beneath those two white throats,
The floor that whirls with dancer's step,
And death's dark notes,
Now tell me—

        Who
Under a stone bridge in the
Darkness?—Wait, the wind, the columned air,
The leaves are falling, and they gather there
Like China's universities before the gate.

Martha's Vineyard

The valleys of this earth patrol the sky;
Her mountains are the mountains on the moon.
Below us here the first white flowers die;
They all will soon.

Greater than life is love, and cannot end
Even in immortality; we take
Dimension from the force which made the moon,
The earth, quake.

Like roses we have seen in early morning
Sweeping a stone wall, spilling upon the ground,
Love creates itself, or, dying small,
Accepts life's wound.

Two and One

Your country is your own, but I inhabit it
With royal privilege, land-grant of light
From our first lord, his majesty, the sun.
In his one eye our worlds are always one,
And differ but, my love, as black from white;
And differ but as ivory from ice,
But as the wind from what the wind has said,
But as the hollow gourd from human head,
But as the morning differs from the night.
Your country is your own, but never yours;
No one singly lives, nor long endures,
But sits with dominoes among the dead,
But sits below the earth by caverned streams;
And works the abdication of the sun,
The absolute negation of the dead,
And brings to nothingness our common dreams.

Still Life

Where no one else at all was sitting,
Mabel sat,
Her fingers flying at her knitting
Like the claws of a cat.

Geraniums were planted
Like Canadian police
While dancers danced in ivory
Along the mantelpiece.

The cat on the piano took
An octave on the keys;
And wind from Tuscaloosa shook
The apple trees.

The hunched and old, anaemic moon,
Orion, and the Dog,
Wander by the cottonwood
In wisps of fog.

Red the wool upon the rug,
The curtains drawn.
Where no one else at all is going,
Mabel's gone.

For a Deaf Angora Cat

The jungle lies about you, and the ground
Is measured by your stealthy step, the sound
Of birds extinct in pure, autumnal flight.
What centuries of breeding, ah, poor dear,
Brought you to your plight like aged Lear
Who struggled on the heath one winter night.

Enough. I follow you beyond the trees
Into the presence of your enemies,
The victims of your superhuman powers.
I find you on a plain whereon there dwell
The antelope, the ostrich, and gazelle,
And tall giraffe that might be speckled flowers.

A wind comes up from nowhere; grasses part
As if to announce a god,—there in the heart
Of darkness stands a Zulu with a spear.
We pay for purity: the heavens burn
With omens, thunder peals; and still you turn
To all, my sweet, your exquisite deaf ear.

Tragedy and Comedy

Two life-sized marble busts of bearded men,
One shoulder draped, the other shoulder bare;
Between the two, like some bright-clad corsair,
The sunlight playing on the frames of gold
Sets free the prisoners the mirrors hold,
And joins the wind across the cold parterre.

No violin need sound; for now no more
Will tufted silk and satin sweep the floor,
Nor logs be heaped upon the roaring flames.
From swans' hooked necks a chandelier descends,
And clothes the ghostly dancers in its flames,
The dancers as they glide along the stair.

Put out the light, the lovely evening ends;
An owl hoots, and rain comes down the skies.
Two lifeless men: one laughs, the other cries,
And facing where the dancers all have fled
Below the balcony, the cold parterre,
Across the dark they both salute the dead.

Marine

A boat is cutting into the sea,
The children all cry, "Look!"
Earth and air are closing in
Like the pages of a book.

The day is brighter than hammered tin,
The breeze, a Mexican broom,
Dusts the air, the flying fin;
The gay umbrellas bloom.

Down comes the wave, up goes the gull,
Out goes the fisherman's hook;
Earth and air are closing in
Like the pages of a book.

White is the bone of the parrot fish,
And the jawbone of the whale;
Anemones in a cut-glass dish
Are not so deathly pale.

A hurricane lamp from far away
Burns in the little room;
And the shutters flap like hammered tin;
The distant breakers boom.

On the edge of the rock, the yellow sand,
In the shade of the leaning tower;
The children dream of the sea, the sea,
A blue cut-flower.

Dream

One day in a dream as I lay at the edge of a cliff,
The black water rose, and the children bobbed in the street.
Death with her bonfires signaled the planes to land
Where glass-beaked birds had pecked at my bound feet.

The water's bare hands reached round the base of the cliff,
And my heart cried, "Hope!" and my brain, "There is nothing unknown."
I looked at my charts, and my kingdoms lay buried in sand,
My desiccate body picked clean as a bird's breastbone.

The ships for the west weighed anchor; I watched them depart.
And on what impossible port were their prows then set,
That they moved with a grace defying the mind and the heart,
With tackle of cloud, with decks encumbered and wet?

The air was like chalk; I was nothing. I thought I had
Reached the end of my dream; and I might have if
The waves had not risen and roared, the winds gone mad—
And when I awoke I lay at the edge of a cliff.

Independence Day

For S. H. in his melancholia

Life is inadequate, but there are many real
   Things of beauty here: the flower peddler's cart
Adrift like an island in the city streets,
   The peddler's mare, lifting her mighty hoof
Aware of all that beauty. And the slate
   Where the schoolboy draws his forty-eight
States, ready to make room for the world.
   The sea's enormous wealth; societies
Commemorating blizzards in the North; the small
   White birds in the South where trees are tall
And the hoopsnake bounces downhill like a wagon wheel.

There are real things of beauty; all
   These things were yours. The shadowy
And fabulous quality of the imaginary
   Is presumed; we know it shall
One day take the world. Now the sea
   Has but poor mimic in the shell; a bell
Must free itself of sound, must break with freedom
   To be free. And so you broke, and so you waved
Farewell to us, and turned away
   To a mirror of completion and of certainty,
To clocks that tick, and have no time to tell.

Poems are praise, and poems cannot end.
    There is no answer for we do not ask.
Upon a cliff of sadness the trees bend
    Strangely toward the sea; the end
Is in oneself. O our unsuffering, suffering
    Sick friend, so life is adequate
And you are whole? There are real things of beauty
    Here, and sorrow is our praise. The day
Is bright, the cloud bank white with gulls.
    And while we lie, and watch the ocean roll,
The wind, an Indian paintbrush, sweeps the sky.

A Few Minutes before Sunset

Heir apparent, prince of purest majesty,
His throat a fine and fluent question mark
Of eloquent and almost aquiline intensity,
The swan invades the pool, the polar dark,
And glides into a hall of mirrors, all
Reflecting him: the world is destitute.

Let every eye then follow him forever
Down marble passages, in golden rooms,
Until this work of reverence is done.
All one can remember is a river,
And a mother who must mourn a dear, dead son,
Summer and the swan, the cold, white plumes.

Lachrymae Christi

Let the redbird come to feast.
The cherry-pickers long have ceased,
And I can see their ladders there
All aslant the summer air,
Heavy on the shining trees.
They bear away the jewel box
With steps like fingers winding clocks
That have not ticked for centuries.
Time is dead: there is no time.
No one now can ever climb
The ladder back to that black bough.
One man did, and he is dead;
And all the woods around are red,
And through the trees the redbirds fly,
While the rain falls from the cold sky.

London

Temptation, oh, temptation, sang the singers,
And the river passed them by like Banquo's ghost.
Deliver us from evil, and the river;
All are lost.

Salvation, oh, salvation, sang the singers,
And the ribs that rose and fell were barrel staves;
And I saw beyond the mist, the magic circle,
The hungry waves.

The river like a serpent moved among them,
And mingled, as it coiled upon each eye,
The faint, the dark, the scarcely flowing water,
And the quiet sky.

Death-in-Life is on us, cried the people.
Leaves from Birnam Wood are on the wind.
Holy, holy, holy, sang the singers,
All have sinned.

The stars have disappeared above the city
Like jewels from the crown of Banquo's ghost;
And London Bridge is falling, falling, falling,
Scaled, and crossed.

The Piazza

When all the world was out-of-doors
By those Etruscan sycamores,
The cool and constant fountains played
Against a line of somber towers,
And turned the moments into flowers,
And bore the sun into the shade.

Militant above the crowds
Assembling there the haughty clouds
Like soldiers capped in full parade
Had broken ranks and overrun
The dying yet immortal sun
In robes of glory still arrayed.

The cypresses along the hill
With savage crest and crimson quill
Kept their cryptic copybook;
And while from out the pages came
Sentences inscribed in flame,
The naked earth in silence shook.

The afternoon was like a bell
Of glass from which the hours fell
And broke in pieces as they passed:
The sun is borne into the shade;
Moments, flowers, fountains fade
With all of light in darkness lost.

A Trip across America

Riding the powerful polished rails
Over abandoned Indian trails,
The lady leaves for the lands beyond.

The coastline dims, the pilot boat
Is lost in fog, the liner sails,
Wreathed in handkerchiefs and tears;
The foghorn sounds a tragic note
That lingers when the harbor clears.

Aboard the train the lady goes
Where the cool black-banked Ohio flows,
Monongahela, and the Tennessee,
Valleys in the shape of swallow tails,
Across the level, burning south,
Through towns that rest on cotton bales.

Westward moves upon the plains,
Plateaux where the observer's eye
Sweeps to infinity and back:
Where cornfields drink the April rain
And mountains sway along the track,
And deserts open to the sky,
And lakes go dry, and canyons crack.

Riding the powerful polished rails
Over abandoned Indian trails,
The lady leaves for the lands beyond.

And takes a continent in her arc,
And to the green Pacific comes.
The air is sweet, the night is dark,
And there she stands upon the shore.
Redwood, redwood, sighs the wind,
As if to open up the door
Of paradise itself. The lady speaks;
The night is shaken to the core.

A lady in a purple gown
Walks with pigeons in a park
At Golden Gate: the shadows move
Below the hills, the voices drown.
So every evening comes to dark,
And all our journeys end in love.

THE WORLD BELOW
THE WINDOW

(1957)

The World below the Window

The geraniums I left last night on the windowsill,
To the best of my knowledge now, are out there still,
And will be there as long as I think they will.

And will be there as long as I think that I
Can throw the window open on the sky,
A touch of geranium pink in the tail of my eye;

As long as I think I see, past leaves green-growing,
Barges moving down a river, water flowing,
Fulfillment in the thought of thought outgoing,

Fulfillment in the sight of sight replying,
Of sound in the sound of small birds southward flying,
In life life-giving, and in death undying.

American Primitive

Look at him there in his stovepipe hat,
His high-top shoes, and his handsome collar;
Only my Daddy could look like that,
And I love my Daddy like he loves his Dollar.

The screen door bangs, and it sounds so funny—
There he is in a shower of gold;
His pockets are stuffed with folding money,
His lips are blue, and his hands feel cold.

He hangs in the hall by his black cravat,
The ladies faint, and the children holler:
Only my Daddy could look like that,
And I love my Daddy like he loves his Dollar.

Lovebirds

Above finespun, unruffled sheets
Bright agitated parakeets
Do not well, encaged, endure
The changes in room temperature.

Heraldic in unstable air,
They seem inclined, impelled to share,
Through active beaks, frayed, busy wings,
Intense concealed imaginings.

They gaze beyond hot coiling pipes
And waving cloth of zebra stripes,
Past thicket-green, plum-colored walls;
Ape incantations, and bird calls,

To where abed, with swift intake
Of breath, the couchant lovers wake,
Muscles tensing, eyes agleam,
Within the alcove's rising steam.

Quadruped, engaged, complete,
The bodies there grotesquely meet
Until with dumb, direct transaction
They end in mutual satisfaction.

Above the tumbling, milk-white sheets
The red-green ruffled parakeets
Do not chatter, do not sing,
But perch, head beneath one wing,

Nor lift their eyes and gaze about
Upon the scene of such a rout;
How can rumpled feathers measure
Such accomplishment of pleasure?

While sated lovers lie apart,
Each sullen still-ballooning heart
Wanders high above their bed
To say requited love is dead.

Love, indeed, no longer here,
Mushrooms into the atmosphere
Until by some celestial curse
It breaks upon the universe.

It breaks—and planets on their round
Wheel unconcerned above the ground;
Winds attack hunched apple trees
And furrow, snakelike, foaming seas.

The bed is made. The parakeets
Flash far away through tropic streets
In and out through black lianas,
Over broad sun-drenched savannahs,

Free and easy as the swing
And sweep of love's imagining
To where the temperature is even,
And the pure sunlight is all from heaven.

Tulip

A slender goblet wreathed in flame,
From Istanbul the flower came
And brought its beauty, and its name.

Now as I lift it up, that fire
Sweeps on from dome to golden spire
Until the East is all aflame:

By curving petals held entire
In cup of ceremonial fire,
Magnificence within a frame.

Nightwood

Seeking in squalor lean, elusive youth,
The pale quean haunts the bars, the murky streets,
Moving from love to love to love to love,
And loving but the self that Love defeats:

And loving but the robin and the wren
That hop from stone to stone on splintered legs,
And do not touch the hearts of buried men,
While clothed in soft, white light, the dark wolf digs.

Letter

Because a stamp will bear the damp
An envelope will bear a stamp.

Stamp and envelope unite
And fly together through the night

To reach the empty letterbox
A lean, uncertain hand unlocks.

Confronted with the cruel prose
Which stamp and envelope enclose,

Distraught, a young man bolts his door,
Paces up and down the floor

While metal rollers cross his brain
One hundred times, and then again,

Until as if congealed entire,
He kneels before a blazing fire

And sinks a knife into his heart.
Stamp and envelope depart:

Wet with tears, they rise in flame,
Leaving no address or name—

Only saffron ash that curls
Around dissolving blue ink-swirls,

Relinquishing to dark alone
Words written by the wind on stone.

Rear Vision

The cars in the mirror come swiftly forward,
While I, in thought, move slowly back;
Time past (reflected) seems to wind
Along the boundaries of mind,
A highway cold, distinct, and black.
Who knows to what the years have led,
And at which turning up ahead—
On the white-stitched road reflected back—
The furies gather in a pack,
While all the sky above burns black,
Unwinding still the darkening thread?

Death of a Jazz Musician

I dreamed that when I died a jukebox played,
And in the metal slots bright coins were laid;
Coins on both my eyes lay cold and bright
As the boatman ferried my thin shade into the night.

I dreamed a jukebox played. I saw the flame
Leap from a whirling disc which bore my name,
Felt fire like music sweep the icy ground—
And forward still the boatman moved, and made no sound.

A Parable

Though well acquainted, Mind and Heart
Are visibly a world apart.

Mind goes blind and takes a tin cup,
Heart with tinsel fills it up.

Heart loses heart one blinding day,
Mind unmindful has little to say.

When Heart and Mind go blind together
And turn in dark to one another,

Mind leading Heart, Heart leading Mind,
Then Love, being blind, will lead the blind

Through fields of mint and golden grain
Into a ditch at the end of a lane;

And there in the ditch the two will lie
Till holes burn slowly through the sky,

And sight restored, they rise and part;
And Mind is Mind, and Heart is Heart.

At the Tombs of the House of Savoy

Turin beneath, on the green banks of the Po,
Lies ringed with bright sunlight, with peaks of snow,
While here in the dark this death's-head wears a crown.
The dead look up, and Death on them looks down,
And bares his teeth, his bone-white haddock eyes,
Which take the casual visitor by surprise
And follow him intently on his round
As fishbone-fine his steps through vaults resound.

The Dressmaker's Workroom

The dressmaker's dummy,
A mute flamingo,
Stands on one leg
For hours just so.

Around it in waves
Skirts billow and swish,
Thin squinting needles,
Slender white fish,

Dart in through shoals
Of blue-black moiré,
Crustacean scissors
Snip slowly away;

Stands while cock feathers
And marabou plumes
Beat the air brightly
Through darkening rooms,

Beads are set tinkling,
Lace makes the sound
Of a small wounded bird
Just grazing the ground,

Gold fringes quiver,
Button eyes stare,
Weird batlike swatches
Weave through the air;

The flamingo reposes,
The garment is sewn,
A shroud that encloses
Bird-feather, bone.

The Ten

. . . one of the best-dressed ten women.

—A newspaper reference
to Mme Henri Bonnet

Mme Bonnet is one of the best-dressed ten;
But what of the slovenly six, the hungry five,
The solemn three who plague all men alive,
The twittering two who appear every now and again?

What of the sexual seven who want only to please,
Advancing in unison down the hospital hall,
Conversing obscenely, wearing no clothing at all,
While under your sterile sheet you flame and freeze?

What will you say of the weird, monotonous one
Who stands beside the table when you write,
Her long hair coiling in the angry light,
Her wild eyes dancing brighter than the sun?

What will you say of her who grasps your pen
And lets the ink run slowly down your page,
Throws back her head and laughs as from a cage:
"Mme Bonnet is one, you say? . . . And then?"

Lion

The lion, ruler over all the beasts,
Triumphant moves upon the grassy plain
With sun like gold upon his tawny brow
And dew like silver on his shaggy mane.

Into himself he draws the rolling thunder,
Beneath his flinty paw great boulders quake;
He will dispatch the mouse to burrow under,
The little deer to shiver in the brake.

He sets the fierce whip of each serpent lashing,
The tall giraffe brings humbly to his knees,
Awakes the sloth, and sends the wild boar crashing,
Wide-eyed monkeys chittering, through the trees.

He gazes down into the quiet river,
Parting the green bulrushes to behold
A sunflower-crown of amethyst and silver,
A royal coat of brushed and beaten gold.

Interior

He took the universe into his room
And shut the door;
Planets circled round his wall,
Stars along the floor
Rose and fell with the grave, slow-breathing dark;
Comets swam like the teeth of the swimming shark,
Beams of oak had monstrous ears,
And jackal's bark.

Sea birds came from distant
Islands; frigates, terns
Preened in the low revolving light
Their sea-bright feathers—wheeling,
Crying, darting down
Toward flickering shoals
Through the long night.

Past and future, two lean panthers
Black as coal,
Paced out the limits of his brain,
His life's veined ore;
And he could see
Gates opening before him quietly
Upon a rose-banked carriage waiting in the rain.

Snow

Late in the day the soft snow comes
To the hungry sparrows like bread crumbs
Where the cold clear lakes are kettledrums.

A drunken workman staggers past
While, drawn to ambush in the west,
The cutthroat sun is failing fast.

A frozen harp, the willow leans
By the water's edge; and what life means
Is shown on scrolls and altar screens

Which open wide for all to see,
In the cold clear lake and frozen tree,
The pure design of tragedy.

While oak fires blaze in Gothic halls,
The flames, reflected on the walls,
Loom wild and dark. And the soft snow falls.

A Pavane for the Nursery

Now touch the air softly,
Step gently. One, two . . .
I'll love you till roses
Are robin's-egg blue;
I'll love you till gravel
Is eaten for bread,
And lemons are orange,
And lavender's red.

Now touch the air softly,
Swing gently the broom.
I'll love you till windows
Are all of a room;
And the table is laid,
And the table is bare,
And the ceiling reposes
On bottomless air.

I'll love you till Heaven
Rips the stars from his coat,
And the Moon rows away in
A glass-bottomed boat;
And Orion steps down
Like a diver below,
And Earth is ablaze,
And Ocean aglow.

So touch the air softly,
And swing the broom high.
We will dust the gray mountains,
And sweep the blue sky;
And I'll love you as long
As the furrow the plow,
As However is Ever,
And Ever is Now.

A Green Place

I know a place all fennel-green and fine
Far from the white ice cap, the glacial flaw,
Where shy mud hen and dainty porcupine
Dance in delight by a quivering pawpaw;

Dance by catalpa tree and flowering peach
With speckled guinea fowl and small raccoon,
While the heron, from his perforated beach,
Extends one bony leg beyond the moon.

I know a place so green and fennel-fine
Its boundary is air; and will you come?
A bellflower tinkles by a trumpet vine,
A shrouded cricket taps a midget drum.

There blue flies buzz among the wild sweet peas;
The water speaks: black insects pluck the stream.
May apples cluster there by bearded trees,
Full-skirted dancers risen from a dream.

Birds call; twigs crackle; wild marsh grasses sway;
Will you come soon, before the cold winds blow
To swirl the dust and drive the leaves away,
And thin-ribbed earth pokes out against the snow?

Robert Frost: The Road Taken

The poet stopped on the edge of night,
   And the road through dark wound on.
Black trees arose; the wind was still;
Blind skeletal walls inched over the hill
   In the mole-gray dawn.

He thought of the way by which he had come,
   Mastered through long years—
Tangles of form and substance, dense
Thickets past which with experience
   A writer steers.

He gazed beyond the familiar night
   On the reasons reason curbs—
Adjectives which say too little,
Adverbs that flare, or with dust settle
   On shining verbs.

A dim house ahead, a journey completed,
   Out of darkness, dawn.
The blind walls move: his words awaken
Here on the page; and the road taken
   Winds on.

Three

"We've gone as far as I think we three can go,"
The Man in the Mirror looked at me and said.
"When I look out I look at the land, Land ho!
When I look out I look at the land ahead. . .

"And O the land is Death," said the Mirror Man.
"The hills come down like glass to the curving sea;
The crystal shallows gaze upon the sun,
The sea reflects the land; the land, the sea."

Two selves I saw. The darker one that spoke
Stood in a frame of unreflecting calm
Against the autumn light, the land of Death,
No land, no self, no sea, no sand, no palm.

Spoke, and was gone. Where three had been were two;
And the mirror whirled as on the sea a raft
Turns and turns. . . . Or was there only one
Who bent his head and touched his hat and laughed?

Processional

The Professor strolls at dusk in the college garden,
And the hollyhocks are blooming, pink and red;
And a delicate wind is blowing, forever blowing,
In and out of the trees and through the Professor's head.

The leaves announce themselves like girls at a party,
The blades of grass stand up all fresh and trim,
While over them swing the cold, fat-bellied shadows,
And the wind goes on rehearsing an evangelical hymn.

Retrace your steps, Professor. The wind in the branches
Blows stronger than even the Devil himself would wish.
The sun sinks low, the great beaked clouds assemble,
And pebbles gleam in the dark like the scales of a tropical fish

And now by rush-filled pools the witches gather;
For this is the night the booming frogs foretell
When beauty will be destroyed by more than weather,
By more than the idiot wind that rakes the pits of hell.

In Memoriam Wallace Stevens

One summer day a blackbird sang
Perched on the back of a great white whale;
Beautiful things by nature fail.

The whale submerged; a sudden gale
Swept the coast: the blackbird flew
Away with sunlight on his tail.

Montezuma, the blackbird sang,
Of lost Atlantis spoke the whale;
Only the cold wave sprang to view.

Against that wild and whirling blue,
A small blackbird, a great white whale,
A mariner shrouded in his sail

And all the blue thoughts that he sang
Are things which must by nature fail,
But, being beautiful, are true.

Autumn

The color of stone when leaves are yellow,
Comes the squirrel, a capital C,
With tail atilt like a violoncello,
Comes the squirrel, musically.

Quick, quick, quick, the notes fly
Up, and off the 'cello floats
Over the lawn where children play,
Over matchstick-masted boats

Under way in the lagoon,
Down the steps, the rock walls,
Over a Triton, bearing shells,
Music flows, water falls.

Time, old hunchback, worn and yellow,
Whets his scythe on weathered stone;
While azure mists invade the hollow,
And turkey-red the leaves come down.

Bachelor's-Buttons

Bachelor's-buttons are fine to see
When one is unattached and free,

When days are long and cares are few
And every green field sown with blue

Cornflowers that profusely seem
Attendant on a young man's dream.

Bachelor's-buttons are fine to see
When one knows no frugality;

And splendid to behold again
Lacing a jacket of gold grain,

A border tended by a wife
Who mends the fraying edge of life;

Who fashions in a hundred ways
Bright seams that cut through one's dark days;

Or will until buttons are counted and sold,
And the blue thread breaks, and earth is cold.

The Diver

Down the dark-skinned diver dived
    In the Indian Ocean of my tear,
Tasted salt, and then drowned.

Coral shades him like a tree
    While overhead the waves pound
Cove and cavern piteously.

Life in contradiction lies,
    And friends are by subtraction found:
The raging water fills my eyes.

Wild Country

In cobwebbed caves lie poisoned arrowheads;
The sunlight strikes the water like a gong
Below the tangled trees, the flower beds:
All the clocks in Switzerland are wrong.

A redbird wounds the woodland as it passes,
Shadows dart as lean and quick as knives;
Blood, red blood, is on the parted grasses;
From a granite ledge, a swimmer dives.

Dives, and with a minimum of movement,
Naked-armed divides the crystal pool;
Bubbles rise like sparks struck from a helmet.
Branches sway; the wind blows clean and cool.

Silence; then the thrashing of the water,
The gravel paths are shimmering and dry;
The great white clouds move on as if forever,
And draw a shade against the morning sky.

A Room in the Villa

What is the mirror saying with its 0?
What secret does the still, untroubled surface lock?
What terror told by chair, by unmade bed and bedclothes?
   Now the clock is speaking; hear the clock.

   Hear it tensely ask: Is someone coming?
Did someone just then step into the hall below?
Is someone there upon the stairway, whistling, humming?
   The solemn mirror's mottled, mocking 0,

   Like some black lake, absorbs all things in silence.
A tattered curtain flaps; the coals within the grate
Are kindled to a brief and unremarked refulgence
   While, patient in the eaves, the shadows wait.

The Descent of Orpheus

Phi Beta Kappa Poem, Columbia, 1951

A cockatoo with nervous, quick cockade
Consumes the cones upon a tree of fire
Whose branches cast a giant, trembling shade
Upon the earth, and on the gilded lyre
Of Orpheus, who wanders underground,
And is consumed, and is consumed by fire.

Hear him, O wild singer, as he moves
Below the helmèd hills:
"We cannot live like this, we must empty
Ourselves of living: we must go down
Through Death's blue acres to the roots of things,
Life's darker surfaces, where huge hot springs
Break from stone.
              We must seek Love
At the center of fire."
                    And through a tangled wood,
Past triple-branching flame, he goes.

Knowledge which is powerful will take
Man down those worn rock ways
Below the ground, into the dark god's
Kingdom, fire–dominion:
He must learn,
Like Orpheus, he cannot turn
But turning find
His sweet love vanished, and descend
Where days are nothing, and dreams end,
And broad and burning rivers flow;
And yet must turn,
And turning, ask,
"What shall I do without her?
                    Che farò?"

                    And wanders on
Beyond all light,
From total darkness into night,
Bearing his flaming shield, his lyre.

Here at the cave's gray mouth,
The grave's green edge,
We watch the cockatoo, and cry: Return,
Return to us among the living.
                    O so much
Is lost with every day: the black vanes
Turn in an angry wind, the roses burn
To ashes on a skeleton of wire;
Sun is mirror to the fire,
And earth, reflected, crumbles at our touch.

THE TALL POETS
Light Verse: Epigrams, Satires, and Nonsense

(1950–1980)

The Tall Poets

A Bicentennial Meditation—July 4, 1976

While the sky above Manhattan flaps with a thousand Jasper Johns,
past file after file of duplicate jubilant faces—
under the glorious gray-green artichoke crown of Liberty,
their free-flowing purple beards catching fire in the morning light
and trailing behind them in wondrous ash-blue wakes
on the welcoming water,
the Tall Poets—in Operation Poetry—
sail up the lordly Hudson.

Manned by the Irish Mafia and the Jewish Mafia
and the Yugoslavian Mafia
(whatever happened to the Sicilian Mafia?)—
a light breeze rippling the fluent free verse of their rigging—
together with the Tall Women Poets,
decked out in tough companionate canvas pants suits,
vulvas cleaving the wind,
the Tall Poets proceed pontifically up the lordly Hudson
on this bright Bicentennial morning.

And there in the mid-Mondrian of Manhattan—
with the boogie-woogie beat of its red white and blue squares—
beside her jade plant and her rubber plant and her Kaffir lily,
beside her innumerable cascading spider plants,
in her Empire chair
beside her Louis Seize commode—
my lady, the lovely long-legged Swan of Strasbourg,
(Yes, Lafayette, she is here)
leans this morning from her white air-conditioned tower,
brooding over the gray water, and she says:

"Where are you, William, why are you not here,
your blue beard billowing above the water,
your majestic *vers libre* ribboning out on the wind—
why are you not here sailing among the Tallest of the Tall Poets—
in Operation Poetry—
up the lordly Hudson?
Why do you dither down there in your dark bayou?
Why do you not let it all hang out
on this bright Bicentennial morning?"

So speaks my beloved, the Swan of Strasbourg,
and I look northward toward her white air-conditioned tower,
and wiping my forehead in the steaming swamp, I answer:
"O my Swan, I wish that I could join you there
in that bright and bugling Bicentennial air—
but my beard, my love,
(the legacy of my Choctaw forebears)
grows solely on my lips and chin
and when it grows I look like Ho Chi Minh
(or did when I was thin)
but now under the TV cameras
my eyebrows disappear—and my beard
becomes a wreath of cobwebs
around a moon-shaped face
until I look like the ghost of Mao Tse-Tung . . .
How wretched and ridiculous I would appear,
sailing up the lordly Hudson there
on this bright Bicentennial morning! . . .

"And besides, I am bored with those Tall Poets,
those first and second generation baby Bunyans,
sick of their creatively written writing,
their blithering buffoonery, their diapered Dada,
their petulant pornography,
their syrupy self-pitying self-interviews,

their admired ash-buried academic anorexia . . .
I'm weary of having to dive into their driven dreck that hits the fan
weekly in every puffed and pompous periodical. . . .
I long for the pure poem,
the passionate statement,
the simple declarative sentence . . .
We live in a bad time . . . and I cannot write . . .
I paddle around this black bayou in my pirogue . . .
Spanish moss hangs from the live oaks like the ash of innumerable
    cigarettes,
and the cypress knees protrude from the black water
like arthritic fingers above a silent typewriter keyboard. . . .
In the dead silence of the bayou a voice deep within me says:
'Walt Whitman is alive and well, and inhabits the Bronx;
he teaches at Stony Brook, and knows exactly what America is thinking.
To hell with rhyme and reason! Walt, unwind! . . . Poor Smith is a hack
overly enamored of writer's block:
he doesn't even know what he thinks until he's said
it; and he has nothing to say.
His mind is as blank as the wobbly whiskered wall-eyed catfish
that he pulled out of the bayou
on this bright Bicentennial morning.'
So says the inner voice while light creaks
down through the rose windows of the cypresses,
and a woodpecker pecks on the dead wood overhead."

From her white air-conditioned tower the Swan of Strasbourg speaks:
"Don't be silly. Stop paddling around in your little pirogue.
Get out of the black backwater of that bayou:
come back up here to the lordly Hudson,
and be the Tall Poet God intended you to be.
Join the other Tall Poets.
Magne-toi le popotin! I didn't marry a piddling paddler of pirogues!"

"Swan," I say, "I know that your great-uncle designed those broad
    avenues in Paris,
and where would we be, I hesitate to say,
without the Champs Elysées?

But I don't feel a bit monumental this Bicentennial morning . . .
Come down, my darling, from your white tower; leave your Louis Seize
    commode
and your Empire chair and your *Compagnie des Indes* china
behind you: come down here to join me in my pirogue,
and together we shall thread our way through the innumerable Louisiana
    bayous
as intricate as the branches of your spider plants—
through the land of my birth—past Dugdemona Swamp and Saline Lake—
past the *Côte joyeuse* and down the Red River like my forebears
past the bearded oaks and the sagging white columns of the plantations
and the writhing black grillwork of Bourbon Street—
through the jubilant notes of early jazz—
and finally out into the glorious Gulf . . . and the light around us
will be pale green—
feathery and fine as stalks of fennel against a background
    of mother- of-pearl,
and when we reach a point unknown on any chart,
and I can say with your Racine,
'The day is no less pure than the depth of my heart,'
I shall begin to write again; and I shall complete that poem begun
a lifetime ago on the edge of the great brown river
on an April morning beside a bank of violets—
a poem of life and death, of love and memory:

"While the Tall Poets—in Operation Poetry—sail up the lordly Hudson,
past the gray contiguous cliffs of the academies,
into the locked and heavily guarded harbors of the anthologies
on this bright Bicentennial morning."

Dead Snake

A gray financier in a thin black auto
Drove over a snake on a country road;
Birds flew up in dust that gathered,
Oak leaves trembled throughout the wood.
Decisive indeed the defeat of Evil;
And inconclusive the triumph of Good.

Light

By television day and night
The people lean to see the light.

The light moves vivid through the air
From Cassiopeia and the Bear,

And everything's as clear as day:
The daughter marries, moves away,

The son grows up, goes off to fight;
A telegram arrives one night

To say he's unaccounted for;
They draw the blinds and bolt the door,

And everything's as clear as day.
The wind comes up, the hemlocks sway,

The light moves vivid through the skies.
They grip the chair and blink their eyes,

And something deep within them throbs;
They set the dial, they work the knobs,

While elephantine shadows fall
And faces leap from the parlor wall.

Plain Talk

"There are people so dumb," my father said,
"That they don't know beans from an old bedstead.
They can't tell one thing from another,
Ella Cinders from Whistler's Mother,
A porcupine quill from a peacock feather,
A buffalo-flop from Florentine leather.
Meatless shanks boiled bare and blue,
They bob up and down like bones in a stew;
Don't know their arse from a sassafras root,
And couldn't pour piss from a cowhide boot
With complete directions on the heel."

That's how *he* felt—that's how *I* feel.

Don Giovanni in Campagna

Giovanni was a lumberjack;
He took delight in fallen trees,
A buxom wench, a smoking stack,
   The small amenities.

In stocking cap of engine red
And shirt of watermelon green,
He loved whatever lay ahead,
   And hated what had been.

Maple, spruce, and gentle pine
He sawed and hacked and hacked and sawed,
While buzzards grazed the timberline,
   And lean wolves crouched and clawed.

He cleared away the virgin trees;
With ax erect he proudly stood
On towering peak; an eerie breeze
   Stirred in the ravaged wood.

He could not move, he could not speak,
He breathed in dust and tasted fire;
The northbound freight's inclement shriek
   Cut through the night like wire.

A buzzard—lank, suspended Z—
Lumbered, swooped; a redwood fell.
Earth divided: John could see
   (Too late) the Pit of Hell.

Epitaphs

A Lawyer

In Memoriam Francis Biddle (1886–1968)

In life each man is tried
And judged at life's expense,
And Time that prosecutes
With such cold competence
Will triumph utterly
Over all humanity,
But, oh, in that great court—
All just men will agree—
How brilliant his defense.

A Greenskeeper

With patient care and subtlety
He ministered to turf and tree:
Gaze now on his green legacy.

A Stripper

Here lies the stripper stripped, disrobed for good;
Death wholly bares what life but partly could.
The house lights dim: each pointed, star-tipped breast
Invites complete approval east and west.

A Small Dog

A Lhasa apso that died fighting with a
Saint Bernard on the coast of Maine

Here Fearless lies: with Asian pride,
Longhaired and small, by the oceanside,
He took up the challenge, fought, and died;
Now hear his bark in the rising tide.

Epigrams

Critic

A short-order cook is the mealymouthed critic,
In his chromium kitchen long has he rambled;
Attacks an egg with a little egg beater
And serves it shirred, or blurred, or scrambled.

"Poet"

After,each,word,he,places,a,comma,
A,remarkable,effect,indeed,
It,gives,you,jitters,when,you,look,
It,gives,you,hiccoughs,when,you,read.

Lady Biographer

She devotes her life to the lives of others,
Sees the poor mad poets as they were;
And how they'd have been if they'd had nice mothers,
Or if they all had married her.

Random Generation of English Sentences or, The Revenge of the Poets

Dr. Louis T. Milic of the Columbia University department of English expressed a note of caution about computers. He said that attention might be diverted to secondary work and that the nature of literature might be distorted if computers changed matters that were essentially qualitative into a quantitative form.

But Professor Milic admitted that computers are improving— perhaps even to the point of writing poetry as good as that composed by a drunken poet. He cited a sentence generated by a group from the Massachusetts Institute of Technology working with a computer, and contained in a study called, "Random Generation of English Sentences."

The sentence is: "What does she put four whistles beside heated rugs for?"

—The New York Times, September 10, 1964

What does she put four whistles beside heated rugs for?
The answer is perfectly clear:
Four drunken poets might reel through the woodwork
And leer.

Four drunken poets might lurch toward the heated rugs,
Bearing buckets of ice,
And say, "Madam, it's colder than your computer may think;
Our advice

Is to pick up your whistles and fold your tents like the Arabs
And silently steal—or fly—
Where all your hot-rugged brothers and sisters are headed.
Madam, good-bye!"

A Tune for the Teletype

O Teletype, tell us of time clocks and trouble,
Wheels within wheels, rings within rings;
In each little ring a pretty wire basket,
In each pretty basket any number of things—

Things to be stamped and dispatched in good order:
O tell us of code clerks and typists who toil
So the world may receive the good news in the morning,
And H-bombs explode according to Hoyle!

H-bombs explode and each pretty wire basket
With bits of charred paper fly off through the air!
The question is answered, but who's there to ask it?
The man with the question is no longer there.

The question-man now is somewhere in orbit;
He's calling—click-click—the whole human race.
A man in the moon, but no cow to jump over—
End of the poem . . . Space . . . Space . . . Space . . . Space . . .

Memorial Day Morning Song

(A Rant)

Honi soit qui Malibu.

—F. Scott Fitzgerald

The bands are playing; flags are out.
    Up, parents, children, pets!
The sun's bright beams flash all about
    Like the legs of majorettes!

The slogans flap; the bugles blare.
    The people wait in waves
Of bunting-hung dramatic bilge
    To decorate the graves.

Up! All together let us sing
    My countrytizathee!
Land of Great Defoliant!
    Land of D.D.T.!

Land of Posh and Prejudice!
    Land of Brave Golf Bag!
Thy Lakes are all of Mercury!
    Thy Cities, Shining Slag!

Thy Deserts glow with Mushroom-Clouds!
  Thy Streams no Fish pollute!
Thy Billy-Graham-Crackers bless
  Thy Manless Flannel Suit!

Thy Belching Stacks! Thy Westward Dreck!
  Thy Jim Crow Toilet Seats!
Thy Zipped-up Corrugated Girls!
  Thy Contaminated Streets!

Thy Homes! Thy Saran-wrap! Thy Foil!
  Thy Plastic-bagged Coleslaw!
Thy Astronauts! Thy Off-shore Oil!
  Thy Whistler's Mother-in-Law!

Land of Nerve Gas! Land of Nixon!
  Land of Bright Beer Can!
Land of Burger! Land of Blivet!
  Land of Great Adman!

From each Remedial Reading Book
  From A to Seussed-up Z
Let Freedom (can you read it?) ring
  From Sea to Oil-swept Sea!

Up, up, up from smog-filled Cave,
  From Babylon, and Bed!
The Jet emits its Anal Wave,
And Warren Harding, from the Grave,
  Will speak for the Glorious Dead!

The Floor and the Ceiling

Winter and summer, whatever the weather,
The Floor and the Ceiling were happy together
In a quaint little house on the outskirts of town
With the Floor looking up and the Ceiling looking down.

The Floor bought the Ceiling an ostrich-plumed hat,
And they dined upon drippings of bacon fat,
Diced artichoke hearts and cottage cheese
And hundreds of other such delicacies.

On a screened-in porch in early spring
They would sit at the player piano and sing.
When the Floor cried in French, *"Ah, je vous adore!"*
The Ceiling replied, "You adorable Floor!"

The years went by as the years they will,
And each little thing was fine until
One evening, enjoying their bacon fat,
The Floor and the Ceiling had a terrible spat.

The Ceiling, loftily looking down,
Said, "You are the *lowest* Floor in this town!"
The Floor, looking up with a frightening grin,
Said, "Keep up your chatter, and *you* will cave in!"

So they went off to bed: while the Floor settled down,
The Ceiling packed up her gay wallflower gown;
And tiptoeing out past the Chippendale chair
And the gateleg table, down the stair,

Took a coat from the hook and a hat from the rack,
And flew out the door—farewell to the Floor!—
And flew out the door, and was seen no more,
And flew out the door, and *never* came back!

In a quaint little house on the outskirts of town,
Now the shutters go bang, and the walls tumble down;
And the roses in summer run wild through the room,
But blooming for no one—then why should they bloom?

For what is a Floor now that brambles have grown
Over window and woodwork and chimney of stone?
For what is a Floor when the Floor stands alone?
And what is a Ceiling when the Ceiling has flown?

Bay-breasted Barge Bird

The bay-breasted barge bird delights in depressions
And simply flourishes during slumps;
It winters on hummocks near used-car lots
    And summers near municipal dumps.

It nests on the coils of old bedsprings,
And lines its nest with the labels from cans;
It feeds its young on rusty red things,
    And bits of pots and pans.

The bay-breasted barge bird joyfully passes
Where bulldozers doze and wreckers rumble,
Gazing bug-eyed, when traffic masses,
    At buildings that feather and crumble.

It wheels and dips to the glare and thunder
Of blasted rock and burning fuel
While the red-hot riveted sun goes under
    On every urban renewal.

It flaps long wings the color of soot,
It cranes a neck dotted with purple bumps;
And lets out a screech like a car in a crack-up
    As it slowly circles the dumps.

Flight of the One-eyed Bat

The night has a thousand eyes,
  The one-eyed bat but one
Which it opens as it flies
  Straight at the setting sun.

Straight at the sun it flies,
  The sun that slowly sinks;
Night blinks its thousand eyes,
  The bat's eye never blinks

But enlarges while it flies
  And jerks its webbed black wings
Like the ribs of an old umbrella
  Or the coils of old bedsprings;

Flies over rooftops and chimneys,
  Over graveyards and hotels,
While factories blow their whistles
  And churches toll their bells;

Flies till the spotlight's extinguished,
  A ruby curtain rung down,
Till the town has clutched at the country,
  And the country swallowed the town;

Flies till the moon's on a clothespin,
  Till the Milky Way dangles from wire,
Till the cat creeps out of the coal bin,
  And the kettle sings by the fire;

Flies till its mission's accomplished,
  A head-on dark deed done:
Night opens a thousand eyes,
  The bat closes one.

The Antimacassar and the Ottoman

"I am leaving this house as soon as I can,"
Said the Antimacassar to the Ottoman.
"I hate this room, I loathe this chair,
I can't stand people's oily hair,
I long for a breath of mountain air.
　I will fly away to Turkistan;
　　Will you come with me, dear Ottoman?"

The Ottoman sighed and said, "Oh, man!
I will certainly go with you if I can.
I, too, am sick of this overstuffed chair
And want nothing more than a breath of air!
I'm weary of having my praises sung
By an ugly pot of Mother-in-law's tongue!
Give me a mountain's twisted shapes
For the arsenic green of those green drapes;
Give me the green of a foreign land
For the green of that green umbrella stand!
I daily see a dreadful menace
In that awful painted scene of Venice
That glows at night like dead desire
Above an artificial fire.
I know by heart the sad tweet-tweets
Of those pale sky-blue parakeets!
And all I can hear is a high-pitched snicker
From that chaise longue of painted wicker!
The African violets are wet,
They haven't dried their pink eyes yet;
Day after day their hot tears come
Across the cold linoleum!
They *loathe* this room as much as I!
　Tears, idle tears! *I* cannot cry.
　　Do let us go—do let us fly!"

But an Ottoman it cannot fly,
And an Antimacassar—who knows why?—
Is pinned in permanence to a chair.
So when morning came, they both were there;
And no window opened to let in the air,
    And neither had flown to Turkistan—
    The Antimacassar nor the Ottoman.

The Typewriter Bird

The Typewriter Bird with the pitchfork beak
Will sing when its feathers are given a tweak,
Will sing from now till the end of the week
In the typewritten language that typewriters speak,
    The Typewriter Bird.

Ugly and clickety, cheerful, and gay,
Skyscraper-blue or tenement-gray,
It hops up and down in its rotary way
And sings till the bell rings, Hip-Hooray!
    The Typewriter Bird.

The Typewriter Bird with the spotted fan
Flies off to the jungles of Yucatán,
Where perched on a table of old rattan,
It sings like water that drips in a pan,
    The Typewriter Bird.

It sings like water Drip-Drop! Drip-Drop!
That falls on a corrugated iron rooftop,
In a round tin pan on the wobbly rattan—
Drip-Drop! Jim-Jim! Drip-Drop! Drip-Drop!
    The Typewriter Bird.

The Typewriter Bird is a terrible bore;
It sings—Jim-Jim—and it sings encore.
It sings in London and Singapore;
It flies to the ceiling, it drops to the floor,
It bangs on the wall, it knocks at the door,
But thrown out the window, it sings no more,
    The Typewriter Bird!

Mr. Smith

How rewarding to know Mr. Smith,
   Whose writings at random appear!
Some think him a joy to be with
   While others do not, it is clear.

His eyes are somewhat Oriental,
   His fingers are notably long;
His disposition is gentle,
   He will jump at the sound of a gong.

His chin is quite smooth and uncleft,
   His face is clean-shaven and bright,
His right arm looks much like his left,
   His left leg it goes with his right.

He has friends in the arts and the sciences;
   He knows only one talent scout;
He can cope with most kitchen appliances,
   But in general prefers dining out.

When young he collected matchboxes,
   He now collects notebooks and hats;
He has eaten *roussettes* (flying foxes),
   Which are really the next thing to bats!

He has never set foot on Majorca,
   He has been to Tahiti twice,
But will seldom, no veteran walker,
   Take two steps when one will suffice.

He abhors motorbikes and boiled cabbage;
   Zippers he just tolerates;
He is wholly indifferent to cribbage,
   And cuts a poor figure on skates.

He weeps by the side of the ocean,
   And goes back the way that he came;
He calls out his name with emotion—
   It returns to him always the same.

It returns on the wind and he hears it
   While the waves make a rustle around;
The dark settles down, and he fears it,
   He fears its thin, crickety sound.

He thinks more and more as time passes,
   Rarely opens a volume on myth.
Until mourned by the tall prairie grasses,
   How rewarding to know Mr. Smith!

THE TIN CAN
(1966)

Morels

A wet gray day—rain falling slowly, mist over the
   valley, mountains dark circumflex smudges in the distance—

Apple blossoms just gone by, the branches feathery still
   as if fluttering with half-visible antennae—

A day in May like so many in these green mountains, and
   I went out just as I had last year

At the same time, and found them there under the big maples—
   by the bend in the road—right where they had stood

Last year and the year before that, risen from the dark duff
   of the woods, emerging at odd angles

From spores hidden by curled and matted leaves, a fringe of
   rain on the grass around them,

Beads of rain on the mounded leaves and mosses round them,

Not in a ring themselves but ringed by jack-in-the-pulpits
   with deep eggplant-colored stripes;

Not ringed but rare, not gilled but polyp-like, having
   sprung up overnight—

These mushrooms of the gods, resembling human organs
   uprooted, rooted only on the air,

Looking like lungs wrenched from the human body, lungs
  reversed, not breathing internally

But being the externalization of breath itself, these
  spicy, twisted cones,

These perforated brown-white asparagus tips—these morels,
  smelling of wet graham crackers mixed with maple leaves;

And, reaching down by the pale green fern shoots, I nipped
  their pulpy stems at the base

And dropped them into a paper bag—a damp brown bag (their
  color)—and carried

Them (weighing absolutely nothing) down the hill and into
  the house; you held them

Under cold bubbling water and sliced them with a surgeon's
  stroke clean through,

And sautéed them over a low flame, butter-brown; and we ate
  them then and there—

Tasting of the sweet damp woods and of the rain one inch
  above the meadow:

It was like feasting upon air.

The Lovers

Above, through lunar woods a goddess flees
Between the curving trunks of slender trees;
Bare Mazda bulbs outline the bone-white rooms

Where, on one elbow, rousing by degrees,
They stare, a sheet loose-folded round their knees,
Off into space, as from Etruscan tombs.

Slave Bracelets

I

You wore six bracelets—all of silver—and they moved on your
   wrist as you moved,

Catching the light, drawing it endlessly up and down in coils as
   you walked,

Bringing light in from the far corners of the room, bearing it
   in coils, cutting it in discs as you moved,

Peeling silver from mirrors, slicing the shadows; and when you
   held out your arm and drew it back,

The bracelets, tapping one upon the other, broke through the
   pebbled hours,

Slowly composing a pattern of continuing sound that I could follow
   clearly from room to room;

And the constant click of bracelets filled every crevice with silver.

II

A wash of silver! On that balcony overlooking the Caribbean I sat,
   and the water

Was a field of broken blue-green on which clouds massed and hovered
   in corners like paws,

And one triangular sail flitted and dipped, a checkered moth, over
  a crimson patch;

And the waves broke on a fringe of coral reef below, sweeping up
  over a circle of sand,

And the sound of breakers rose over my head, billowing out from the
  triangular tin roof protruding above the water,

Echoing dizzily through the green light; and below on the sand I
  followed the fine print of a crab darting in and out of his
  hole with every wave,

Tracing with each movement a slender radiating web, erased, then
  recomposed;

And again the combers climbed, and again your bracelets with their
  tapping radiantly caught

In the tail of my eye; the sea became a battery of bangles, a
  heap of polished abalone, uncoiling in profusion,

Splintering in silver at the day's dim edges, beached in delight
  upon the afternoon.

III

A fountain of energy had sprung up beneath my feet, and was playing
  through my veins; the island

Moved with the sea breeze; abandoned windmills on the coral hummocks
  turned in the imagination;

The ebony—that tree called "woman's tongue"—rattled its dry pods;

The banana clattered its gaudy green leaves like so many machetes;
  frangipani uplifted its clumps of coral branches;

Palm trees inclined; pawpaws trembled; wheelbarrows of fern, guided by
dark hands, came past

And the island was all in motion, but at rest; the sky, drifting off,
was caught at the edge of a cane field

By a grove of casuarinas, tall and feathery, planted in dark rows to
catch the rain,

Drawing water from the air to return it to the underlying levels of
the porous island,

Sweet water seeping down to rest, shimmering-clear, upon the salt,
filtering out through the cane, emerging in black pools on the blond
sand

So that all the island rested upon water—layer on layer—feeling
upon feeling—buoyant and balanced.

IV

With the continous tapping of your bracelets, I began to compose
a whole category of sinuous objects,

To detail an inventory of coiling images, of chains whose links
rose slowly through consciousness,

Rivers meandering in mystical meadows, columns of smoke
encircling unscaled mountains;

I followed with Australian tribes the parabola of the emu's egg across
the sky—

Saw how, landing far off in a pile of kindling, it set fire to the
sun;

I dug deep beside the legendary Papuan and uncovered with him the
small bright object,

Which, slipping from our hands, climbed into the sky to become the
    moon.

I set out with Dionysus to visit the islands, and abducted with him
    by pirates, was tied with heavy cords

Only to see the knots loosen miraculously and fall to the deck;

Watched the face of the terrified pilot when he sensed that their
    captive was divine,

And the obdurate pirates still refused his release; saw the water
    darken about the ship,

Flowing freely into fragrant wine, while up from the deck, its
    branches enveloping the sail, a vine rose, looping its firm
    trunk around the mast,

And at my side, beneath great pendant clusters, under crisp, veined
    leaves

The god assumed his fearful aspect, and the sailors in horror leapt
    into the sea,

Where, as dolphins, they followed along in the somber water; and
    only the pilot survived.

V

Coils of sound uncoiling, loop on silver loop, circle of light on
    light—

Layer on layer! A crinkling serpent slithered through the shadows,
    nearer and nearer, always eluding me, twisting up through the
    mind's incalculable levels;

And I saw you then, a statuette poised against blue-green water,

A Cretan goddess, whose corsage exposed her small white breasts,
  her lapis lazuli, flounced blue skirts hooped over her waist,

Her arms extending rigidly down before her, serpents of gold and silver
  descending each arm into the resonant shadows,

Each neck held firmly between her fingers, the triangular heads
  thrust upward

—While the triangular tin roof behind you reflected the climbing
  breakers—

Each serpent clasped as if forever, its bright fangs reaching
  resolutely upward, uniting heaven and earth.

The Arrow

If body is a bow, and soul the string,
How certain is the arrow of the eye!
Like Zeno's arrow, held within the tumbling
Wing of time, it flies yet cannot fly
Unless through all eternity it fly
And bring down death, an unrelenting lie,
And being conquered, conquer—and so sing!

Northern Lights

I

I stepped out here on the mountainside, and saw the
    northern lights, cold-clear, clear-white, blue-green, long
    quivering gold knives of light shooting up, cutting the
    sky the horizon round.

Up from the valley mist rose in waves, shot up in steady puffs,
    clear-cold in the light,

And in places all the sky seemed made of moving skeins of white
    hair rising water-clear, stars tangled in the flowing strands.

The brook ran below (it was August, but cold); and I could hear
    its chill, pebbled water bubbling down, close in upon my ear.

Crickety night sounds: black trees came spangled forth, while
    behind a moving green gold turned them into shaggy hulks
    heaving in waves of light.

Trees stood, but moved, bearded and blowing, but no wind blew,
    and the dark itself moved, kept moving with light.

II

Mist, held deep in the valley in layers chalk-white, sheet-white,
    hung billowing between rock walls;

And still it rose, shade becoming light, light, shade, and as I
    stepped into the field, grass also moved, brightened by all
    these waves of hairy light.

The mountain pool caught, and tried to hold, patches of moving
   light, and the water, coming down from the mountain, rang,
   swinging clear

Over evergreens overgrown; ribbons of willow, beside or behind
   or above the pool, leaned, moved, kept clear-turning until
   the whole sky moved; and I stepped into an ever-deepening
   river of grass, green-moving and slow, glowworm-light
   expanding and wavering.

Thin blades of green cut through blue-green, or green upon white,
   white upon gray, green upon mist-yellow, green and primrose-
   yellow.

And primroses beside the rockpool, chill yellow in the moving
   mist; and light kept coming by while I moved with light
   moving, stood (leapt), reached (held) earth-air (whole-part),
   clear-cold and all-white.

III

I stepped forth, calm but much shaken: no night there ever had
   been so mist-torn, mountain-white.

The Milky Way had broken loose, and spun, a real web, round and
   round until the milk strands tore loose, and hung dangling
   above the valley.

A black dog lay by the road's edge, by a branch from a tree
   fallen, unmoving, shaggy with mist;

The dark barn jutted forth, its peak a prow, against the buffalo-
   humped mountains, and

In all innocence this night broke clear, sailing, sails trimmed
   and taut, no longer beclouded and cloud-tossed, but coming
   through, all clear.

IV

An August night: Jupiter off there in blowing, blissful mist-light.

It was cold; and sheer puffs, seemingly unpropelled, kept
   coming up and out until the whole sky was moving, nacreous
   and white—

All over mother-of-pearl, but pearl yet unformed, not white, but
   blue-rippling pearl-shell, caught up and streaming, moss-green,
   salmon-pink, and shaken.

Drunken, shivering, cold-quaking, I stood, moving skyward, still
   drinking deep draughts shimmering and milk-white.

V

The sky was a moving bowl, hairy and white, with the stars chiseled
   and chipped, spinning in the whole sky.

And the sky was rinsed clear, while the brook rushed on below,
   cleaving night sounds.

And the whole night moved, an upturned bowl, as if the soul itself
   had been washed clear

Of all entanglements, and shone forth, fresh-clean, overturned and
   opalescent.

It was as if the soul alone could speak, and having spoken, rippled,
   rubbed, and crossed, had been drained of speech

And shone forth new-clean, clear-cold, and white, with nothing
   now within to hold or hide . . .

And I brushed the blowing skeins of light from my face, stepped
   back and shut the door and went inside.

The Idiot below the El

From summer's tree the leopard leaves are torn
Like faces from the windows of the train,
And at my foot a mad boy's tweed cap falls,
And no moth's born that can disturb his brain.

The traffic, with a sound of cap and bells,
Winds into his ear; his blunted eyes
Are buttonhooks, his tight lips twisted shells,
His fingers, candy canes to snare the flies.

Below, the leaves lie still in wind and rain,
And overhead the rails run on and meet
Somewhere outside of time: the clamor dies;
An iron hoop goes clanking down the street.

Where the Rivers Meet

*On the Inauguration of Thomas Hopkinson Eliot as
Chancellor of Washington University
12 October 1962*

Here where the winding rivers meet,
What is it that the autumn air,
So full and fine, so bittersweet,
   Would clearly now declare?
Queen Anne's lace and goldenrod
That grace this bright Columbus day—
Unto what glory do they nod?
   What have they now to say?
The regal pheasant, dove, and quail,
The cardinals and flashing jays,
Met with on an Ozark trail—
   What is it now they praise?

Those rivers that no dark can dim—
The Meramec, the Gasconade—
Where summer-long I used to swim,
   And other boys now wade;
That gravel bank, that clear, cold spring,
Where, shaded, pensively I sat
And fished for crawfish on a string
   With strips of bacon fat;
Those lean-tos built of sassafras,
Tents pitched with wobbly sumac poles,
Those caverns reached through fern and grass
   By frightening sinkholes,—

Remembered places that I see,
Persimmons ripened on a bough,
But riper now in memory—
    What have they to avow?
St. Louis, birthplace of the blues,
Of T. S. Eliot, Eugene Field,
Producer of good beer and shoes,
    Of Prophets unrevealed,
St. Louis, you whose every haunt
I used to know—your parks, your drives,
The shanties on your riverfront,
    Your mansions and your dives,—

City, whose spirit once possessed
Charles Lindbergh the moment he
Brought his rickety plane to rest,—
    What would you have us see?
City, whose every thoroughfare—
Broadway and Olive, Delmar, Grand—
Leads to that central fountain, where,
    A flower in his hand,
Mississippi strides to meet
Missouri, nude in open court,
While windblown fans of spray compete,
    And water-folk cavort,—

Streets that are named for Lafayette,
Pierre Laclede, Auguste Chouteau,
What would you have us not forget,
    What would you let us know?
Streets that I traveled early, late,
And now but faintly recognize,
What is it that they celebrate,
    What do they emphasize?
Remembered streets and fields and flowers,
The rich, rewarding out-of-doors,—
All announce this day is ours,
    This day, our Chancellor's.

And those who have assembled here
To wish him health, long life, and fame,
The red and green of autumn wear,
  To glorify his name;
So may this day of fine converse
In festive hood and somber robe
Be the pivot of their universe,
  The center of their globe;
May winter snow and autumn rain
Be all clear weather on their chart;
Reward them with a fertile brain
  And understanding heart.

May they probe wisdom's deepest worth,
The flood of learning never stem,
That they may honor him henceforth
  Who this day honors them.
May every mind and heart explore
The space expanding with the stars
That illuminate this muddy shore,
  These willow-banked sandbars;
And may they brighten all his days
Until each eye enlightened greet
The Chancellor, whom now we praise
  Here where the rivers meet.

Marcel Proust

His childhood he gave to a public which had none,
And then withdrawing to a cork-lined room,
Lived ever after . . . On his pages sprawl
Sentences like vine leaves on the wall
Of some well-weathered ruin where the sun
Picks out the childlike letters on a tomb.

An Observation

For Marianne Moore on her seventy-seventh birthday

Now every day here at the height of summer
   from the edge of the apple tree bent by
   the weight of its fruit so that the whole thing

Is crisscrossed with strings of small green apples,
   looped every which way up and down and in and
   out—

Through the midday haze against the mountains swathed
   now in a gray-blue gauze of heat—

From the heart of the apple tree, its bark mottled and
   warped, its branches hooked and looking half-
   hollow—

From the hunched and dwarfed apple tree, and then from
   deep within the gray-green of the swamp willow—
   as if on a scale up and down its trailing
   branches—

Then high there on the bough of the fat bulging ash, its
   gold keys hanging dry and desperate like the fringe
   of old upholstery—

Now every day when all the other birds and even the
   insects have ceased I hear his chip-chip sweet-sweet
   chew-chew, followed by what sounds like a high *wit*—

Wit—which, as you know, somehow cuts through the heart
   of haze; and see him—a blue gem

Resting within the gray cushions of heat—his blue turning
   in the half-hooded light from indigo to ultramarine
   to azure,

Drawing into his faceted feathered body the gold and olive
   green of the mountains, absorbing as in watercolor all
   the lost color of the heavens

While below him dragonflies beside the elderberry bush dart
   their wild blue brooches over the wet velvet surface of
   the pond;

See him as you would see him, this New England visitor from
   the coast of Cuba, this indigo bunting as more than a
   mere jewel—

As a flame breathing at the core of consciousness, fed by
   conscience, a poem poised against the shifting dull
   gray seasons, asking, in its permanence and rare
   felicity, "What are years?"

Petits Chevaux: The Twenties

I

Harry Crosby one day launched the Bedroom Stakes—
Frivolity out in front, Fidelity overtaken by Concubine.
The play was fast, the bets were high. Who lost? Who won?
Green baize drank the tilting shadows of the sun,
And Death left the players' goblets brimming with blood-red wine.

II

Scott Fitzgerald organized the Crack-up Stakes—
The horses galloped ahead; Victrola records turned.
He downed his drink and wrote; wife Zelda whirled and swayed;
The goblets shattered, but the words survived Time's raid,
And Zelda danced on madly till the asylum burned.

The Tempest

Let England knowe our willingnesse, for that our worke is goode,
Wee hope to plant a Nation, where none before hath stood.

—R. RICH in *Newes from Virginia*

Imagine that July morning: Cape Henry and Virginia
There but one week off; black winds having gathered
All the night before,
The gray clouds thickened, and the storm,
From out the wild Northeast, bore
Down upon them, beating light from heaven.
The cries of all on board were drowned in wind,
And wind in thunder drowned;
With useless sails upwound,
The Sea Adventure rode upon rivers of rain
To no known destination.
Bison-black, white-tongued, the waves
Swept round;
Green-meadow beautiful, the sea below swung up
To meet them, hollow filling hollow,
Till sound absorbed all sound;
Lashed about gnatlike in the dark,
The men with candle flame
Sought out the leaks along the hull.

While oakum spewed, one leak they found
Within the gunnery room, and this they stopped
With slabs of beef;
Their food they fed that leak, that wound,
But it continued still to bleed, and bled
Until its blood was everywhere,
And they could see their own blood
Rush to join it,
And the decks were wet and red;
And greater leaks sprang open in the hold.

Then, on the fourth day, having given up
All but themselves the ship contained—
Trunks, chests, food, firearms, beer and wine—
When they prepared to hack
The mainmast, to batten down all hatches
And commit the vessel to the sea,
They saw far off—sweet introduction of good hope—
A wavering light-green, brooding calm,
Trees moving with the waves—and it was land.

And so the ship rode on, rode out the gale,
And brought them, wrecked but living, to the island there,
Where safely, under more compliant skies,
They might chart out that voyage to a shore
On which the nation they had planted would in time arise.

Fisher King

The tall Fijian spears a giant turtle
And hurls him down upon the foaming breakers;
Then rides him over gardens green and fertile
Past huge marine toadstools and pepper-shakers.

What elegance in that superb design,
What native mastery of nerve and eye!
Along the shore, a plumed and nodding line
Of fine-ribbed, slender palm trees flanks the sky.

The waiting island there, an open leaf,
Hangs trembling on the waves, the heavens crack;
While breakers climb the bone-white coral reef,
Triumphantly he rides the ocean back.

So seeing him, I see again at dawn,
Beyond the shifting boundaries of night,
His image, from the dark unconscious drawn,
Come shimmering and powerful to light.

The Angry Man

El sueño de la razón produce monstruos.

—GOYA

I

Reason slumbers; and in the terrible isolation of my anger I observe
  a thousand monsters of the mind's making;

I wander on a moonscape exploring its tunnels, picking up bits and
  pieces of the past

To hurl at growling beasts that sulk away half-seen; I gaze from a
  steel cage out at a wall rimmed with dragons' teeth,
  observation towers and aprons of barbed wire

Lacing the horizon; eyes peer through the night as through the
  isinglass of old coal stoves;

I am a passenger on a ship in the shape of a carving block
  bearing a cargo of bones;

I know the language spoken by cats and dogs, all peripheral tongues;
  I invent new words, every syllable detailing disaster;

I am the King of Buttons, enriched by bottle-caps, profligate with
  paper;

My voice goes out like a funicular over an abyss, and my hands
  hang at my side, clenching the void;

My dreams are filled with bitter oranges and carrots, signifying
     calumny and sorrow;

And when I awake the windows are outlined in creosote; a network
     of pipes is thrown up around my room and water pours from
     a yellow geyser in the plaster.

II

Reason slumbers; and I go where the world takes me—back upon
     myself; and if I have slept, I awake, projected on a raft
     into a soft green landscape

Where blanched concrete highways keep circling the hillsides in
     whalebone, drinking up the cars through the baleen formed by
     spiny trees against the sunset—

And I am the passenger hurled from the passing car, the driver
     swallowed by the black whale of the world;

And the journey ends where it began: the black whale's mouth opens
     around me into a pleated camera in which my eye is the lens—

And what I see is a world opening into other black mouths—
     gullet to gullet—lens to lens—

And what is recording is recorded, what is seeing, seen; and
     the giant shutter opens always on horror.

III

The monsters of the mind's making have begun their destruction
     and will carry it through;

They keep attacking, throwing iron hoops that encircle my
     ankles, thighs, chest

Until I am bound with iron rope and hung from a precipice; and the
  cliff is no cliff but a ceiling from which hairy roots
  dangle at my side—

Not roots but the branches of trees growing into the air by their
  roots—

Around them dream flowers twisting out—black roses, blue sun-
  flowers following a black sun—

Morning glories, dirt-colored blooms encircling mansarded
  basements—

Skylights opening out like trapdoors into gray cloud caverns in
  which birds dive downward like fish, and television aerials float,
  the skeletons of dangling kites—

Rivers are nailed above me, their bird-fish flying, teeth dragging
  the marbled water, and their debris lining a painted dome of
  tin cans, bottles, rusted and twisting knives;

A bloated piano like a black armadillo bores its way over the
  edges into a cloud

And cemeteries drift overhead like upturned trays held by frozen
  waiters.

IV

The black iron hoops snap and uncoil, coiling me upward, upright,
  backward in time and space;

I am alone in a courtyard in the middle of a desert, holding in my
  hands the coils that have become a whip.

It is dusk, and the air is alive with soft flying creatures;
  I snap the whip at them, looping their bodies, bringing
  them down until the stones of the courtyard are red

And at last the air is quiet and no chirp or whimper is heard
  from any chink or crevice.

I climb the spiral stone steps to a room overlooking the desert;
  and I lie now on an iron cot watching the moon-white sand
  billow out in waves like the sea;

And the whip, having answered unreasoning reason, rests limp
  at my side—a tassel, a tail, a reed.

A Picture of Her Bones

I saw her pelvic bones one April day
After her fall—
Without their leap, without their surge or sway—
I saw her pelvic bones in cold X ray
After her fall.
She lay in bed; the night before she'd lain
On a mat of leaves, black boulders shining
Between the trees, trees that in rain pitched every which way
Below the crumbling wall,
Making shadows where no shadows were,
Writing black on white, white on black,
As in X ray,
While rain came slowly down, and gray
Mist rolled up from the valley.
How still, how far away
That scene is now: the car door
Swinging open above her in the night,
A black tongue hanging over
That abyss, saying nothing into the night,
Saying only that white is black and black is white,
Saying only that there was nothing to say.
No blood, no sound,
No sign of hurt nor harm, nothing in disarray,
Slow rain like tears (the tears have dried away).
I held her bare bones in my hands
While swathed in hospital white she lay;
And hold them still, and still they move
As, tall and proud, she strides today,
The sweet grass brushing her thighs,
A whole wet orchard mirrored in her eyes;—

Or move against me here—
With all their lilt, their spring and surge and sway—
As once they did that other April day
Before her fall.

Riddles

I

Within a frame in narrow tinkling strands,
Down-rippling on the body, through the hands,
It hangs as if dividing life from death:
Approach it now, and part it with your breath.

2

In glass contained, and gnawed as if by doubt,
Its tongue uncoiled to drive the shadows out,
How serpent-like upon the crackling air
It broods upon a page of Baudelaire!

3

It dogs your footsteps through the sunny day
Till night comes down and spirits it away;
Lengthening with light, it takes you whole,
Becomes your body and assumes your soul.

4

Earth it rounds with heaven's bloom—
A round of earth in a sunlit room.

5

It leads you a chase through a tangle of words
And gives but the bones when you look for the birds.

ANSWERS: *1. Bead Curtain; 2. Oil Lamp; 3. Shadow;
4. Flowerpot; 5. Riddle*

The Woman on the Porch

A woman in my dream sits on a cool front porch,
And there, through the declining afternoon,
Weaves within her mind the threads of my story,
Calling the characters in from the shadows.

Then, weary of conjuring,
As if this light, half-light,
Were in itself too great
To bear, and she were drawn onstage
Before the most receptive of audiences,
She leaves behind my half-completed story,
And walks across the green
Front lawn to the flower beds.

Bending above them,
Her eye catching the sun's last flames,
She says: "Flowers are children; when
I see them I want to know their names . . ."

And the flowers answer
And identify themselves—
Rose, carnation, sunflower, camellia,

While night comes down within my dream upon the world,
And the sky, for a brief moment, is the color of currant and quince.

Dachshunds

The deer and the dachshund are one.

—WALLACE STEVENS, "Loneliness in Jersey City"

The Dachshund leads a quiet life
    Not far above the ground;
He takes an elongated wife,
    They travel all around.

They leave the lighted metropole;
    Nor turn to look behind
Upon the headlands of the soul,
    The tundras of the mind.

They climb together through the dusk
    To ask the Lost-and-Found
For information on the stars
    Not far above the ground.

The Dachshunds seem to journey on:
    And following them, I
Take up my monocle, the Moon,
    And gaze into the sky.

Pursuing them with comic art
    Beyond a cosmic goal,
I see the whole within the part,
    The part within the whole;

See planets wheeling overhead,
    Mysterious and slow,
While Morning buckles on his red,
    And on the Dachshunds go.

Funeral

Now he is gone where worms can feed
Upon him, a discarded rind,
God's image, and a thinking reed,
    In blindness blind

As any taxidermist's owl.
He who was tall and fleet and fair
Is now no more; the winds howl,
    The stones stare.

Your double who went dressed in black
And beat the lions to their cage
Lies in blood; the whips crack,
    The beasts rage.

Don your somber herringbone
And clap your top hat to your head.
The carriage waits; the axles groan;
    While prayers are said,

Rest your hot forehead on the plush;
And hear, beyond the measured, sad
Funereal drums, above the hush,
    The lions pad

Intently through some sunless glade,
The body's blood-fed beasts in all
Their fury, while the lifted spade
    Lets earth fall.

The Tin Can

One very good thing I have learned from writer friends in Japan is that when you have a lot of work to do, especially writing, the best thing is to take yourself off and hide away. The Japanese have a word for this, the "kanzume," or the "tin can," which means about what we would mean by the "lock-up." When someone gets off by himself to concentrate, they say, "He has gone into the tin can."

—HERBERT PASSIN, "The Mountain Hermitage: Pages from a
Japanese Notebook," *Encounter*, August 1957

I

I have gone into the tin can; not in late spring, fleeing a stewing,
    meat-and-fish smelling city of paper houses,

Not when wisteria hangs, a purple cloud, robbing the pines of
    their color, have I sought out the gray plain, the indeterminate
    outer edge of a determined world,

Not to an inn nestling astride a waterfall where two mountains
    meet and the misty indecisiveness of Japanese ink-drawn pines
    frames the afternoon, providing from a sheer bluff an adequate
    view of infinity.

But here to the tin can in midwinter: to a sagging New England
    farmhouse in the rock-rooted mountains, where wind rifles the
    cracks,

Here surrounded by crosshatched, tumbling stone walls, where
    the snow plow with its broad orange side-thrust has outlined
    a rutted road,

Where the dimly cracked gray bowl of the sky rests firmly on the
  valley and gum-thick clouds pour out at the edges,

Where in the hooded afternoon a pockmarked, porcupine-
  quilled landscape fills with snow-swirls, and the tin can settles
  in the snow.

I have gone into the tin can, head high, resolute, ready to confront
  the horrible, black underside of the world.

Snow-murmur! Wind-dip. Heart-rage! It is now my duty to
  record, to enumerate, to set down the sounds, smells, meanings
  of this place . . .

How begin? With the red eye of the chocolate-brown rhinoceros?
  With the triple-serrated teeth of the pencil-fed monster with
  bright fluted ears and whirling black tail? . . .

There is a skittering and scrambling in the can: a trickle of sand
  and sawdust from a sack, wet leaves blown back, cracks spreading
  along the wall.

There is the chitter and clatter of keys, a smudge of pencils, a
  smear of time . . .

Stippled heaven! Snow-ruffle! Garnet-groove! Black water winding
  through snow-wounds! Ripple-roost!

Will the wilds wake? Will the words work? Will the rattle and
  rustle subside? Will the words rise?

A blue jay flashes by a window, the stripes of his tail, chevrons
  torn from a noncom's sleeve; and in the afternoon the snow
  begins.

First: a hush—pit-stillness, black accent of hemlocks up and down
  the mountain, mist in the valley thickening and deepening
  until it breaks

And the snow already fallen swirls up to meet the snow descending—
   sky-darkening, still-deepening, sky-hooded and whirling,
   flakes flying,

Houses settling sidewise in the drifts—winds wedging, snow-
   choked road lost, still-winding, earth white-star-carpeted, still-
   wheeling;

And in the tin can the same still, paper-white, damp emptiness.

II

A door opens—is it a door?—and a woman walks by in the tin
   can watering tropical plants that jut from the wall or spring
   from the floor, their leaves great green famished mouths,—

Feeding the fish, distributing specks to the seahorses in their tank
   and meat to the turtle on his wet pillow;

Cats curling about her legs, she pats the dogs and caresses the
   heads of the children, and the children open their green mouths
   and grow upward toward the sunlight like plants.

A door opens: a woman walks by, and through her bobbing,
   mud-colored glass watches the movements of my pencil,

And a record turns, a black hemstitched whirlpool, and the
   woman wheels off in a trance of drumbeats, screaming of need
   and nothingness and money;

And money like wet leaves piles high around my ankles, and I am
   sickened by its smell . . .

Snow-madness! Leaf-mania! Green parabolas! In the tin can
   there is no morning of revelation, no afternoon of appraisal, no
   evening of enchantment.

In the tin can a small boy in a nightmare kicks one leg from the
bed overturning a glowing iron stove, and in seconds fire
sweeps through a city of tin cans.

I wake thinking of the boy, and all about me are the smoking
ruins of cigarettes; and the ashes descend through the half-
extinguished afternoon with the smell of burning flesh . . .

A weasel waddles along in a kind of trotting walk; a mole inches
up through darkness, his blind trail, the workings of conscious-
ness.

In the tin can I hear a murmur of voices speaking of the life in other
tin cans, of death sifting through them.

A vision of bodies blasted on the black earth; and I think of those
photographs my father kept from the Nicaraguan Insurrection,
was it?—that we played with as children on a sun-spotted
floor—

Brown bodies spread out over the jungle floor, the figures beside
them wide-eyed and bewildered, toy soldiers in ridiculous stances
in a meaningless world;

I think of the photographs rubbed vinegar-brown in the sunlight;
and of how we placed them around us, lined our toy fortress
with them,

And talked to one another through tin-can telephones, while
from out the photographs the jungle's green arm tapped our
small brown shoulders.

III

The tin can is circling with beasts: dogs howl in the night, cats
sidle through slats in the tin, wet field mice hanging from their
mouths;

I step in the morning over the entrails of rodents lying like spun
    jewels on the carpet, offerings to the dark gods.   .

And the dogs rise from their corners, their dirt-crusted rag beds,
    smelling of snow, sniffing the roots, digging the floor, and
    begin again to circle the can . . .

Bright flashes of morning! Blue snow-peaks! Fog smoking the
    valleys! Angels lighting the rubble! Children skating on a blue
    pond! Deer stepping delicately down through the pines! . . .

And always the face, the woman's face, brooding over all, rising
    from the earth beside me, disembodied; always the woman
    clean and classic as sunlight, moving about the room, sifting
    the dirt, watering the shadowy flowers, polishing the spotted
    tin.

I hear her speak softly; and there she is again beside me; and again
    the face turns, a small bat-face and the lips draw back in a red
    wound and shriek; and the room is filled with a smell of mould
    and money . . .

The woman turns, the bat-face again a woman's face blue with
    shrieking, and the woman walks to the end of the corridor,
    climbs a broad white stairway . . .

Leaf-fringe! Sky-tingle! Cloud-clatter! Earth-blaze! All my under-
    world crumbles; and I am left with the one brooding face,
    no face; with bat-wings folding the black air into a shroud.

IV

When am I to emerge? Dirt falls; eyes blur; memory confounds;
    multiple voices move furred and batlike round my ears; and
    then no sound—

Only the grating of a pencil over a page—an army of ant words
    swarming up to consciousness.

When will they break through to a bright remembered world, up
through the top of the tin?

Snow-swirl—hemlocks hunching toward the window—gray-
black shadow cutting over black, fan shaken over fan . . .

From here the windows open their white mouths to swallow the
wind-driven snow.

And I remember salmon sky, fine-boned sunsets sweeping the
spiny mountains; and I have seen the snow

In banks driven back from the road, the black edges scraggly and
bearded, the snowbanks under the birches like milk from
buckets overturned and frozen . . .

Will the words rise? Will the poem radiate with morning? Here
where I see nothing, I have seen the Cyclops-eye ballooning
over a frozen world,

The wide fringe of eyelashes opening on all existence, the single
glazed dazzle of the eye watching,

And I have lived with my eyes—watching the watching eye, the
eyeball swiveling in nothingness, a huge black moon in egg-
white immensity.

And I have seen the edges of the tin can fold in around it.

V

O bodies my body has known! Bodies my body has touched and
remembered—in beds, in baths, in streams, on fields and streets
—will you remember?

Sweet vision of flesh known and loved, lusted after, cherished,
repulsed, forgotten, and remembered, will you remember my
body buried now and forgotten? . . .

In childhood we played for hours in the sun on a dump near a
    cannery; and the long thin ribbons of tin rippled round us,
    and we ran by the railroad track and into the backyard behind
    the asparagus and through the feathers of green our bodies
    touched and the strips of tin radiated their rainbows of light—

And our bodies were spiraled with tin and wondrous with light—

Now out of darkness here from the tin can, through snow-swirl
    and wind-dazzle, let the tin ribbons ride again and range in
    newfound freedom;

Let the tin rip and rustle in the wind; let the green leaves rise and
    rift the wondrous windows, leaving behind the raging women,
    and the sickening mould of money, rust, and rubble . . .

And the words clean-spun and spiraling orbit that swift-seeing,
    unseen immensity that will never be contained!

WHAT TRAIN WILL COME?
(1966–1980)

Hull Bay, St. Thomas

For Jay and Ann Logan

We come, with a busload of children, nervous from the heat, down
through lush vegetation, green from recent rain,

Down from Drake's Seat, from which the explorer must have seen
the other Virgin Islands as they are now, perched below him
in blue-green water,

Past palmetto, banana, and brown-podded flamboyant, down to
cool, yellow-brown sand under a mango tree;

And the children flee from the bus and fan out, a scattering of
hot seed, over the sand;

Come to a scene straight from an old print, black rocks jumbled
and jutting ahead into the sky,

A full red sun setting slightly to the left of the rocks, the bay
fringed with a steady surf, dark above, white beneath,

Spray flung back at the far corners of blue-black rock amid an
unraveling of pink clouds;

And all that is missing is a high-prowed frigate anchored in the
foreground, sails furled, its armored captain stepping
daintily into his boat;

The children, lost sight of like the absent frigate, find
   their own abandoned boat high on the sand under the mango,
   and tumble over its gun-gray gunwales like exhausted birds;

Their cries are muffled by the sound of birds sweeping through
   the air, gliding slowly in, plopping onto the water,

Pelicans with ludicrous long beaks like tilted shears, or, half-
   opened, like garden trowels escaped from the hands of a
   mad gardener,

Pelicans circling, diving—one, two, three at a time—the
   silly beak become a blade,

A surgeon's scalpel, expertly wielded, cutting through the
   delicate green flesh of the water right to the fish below—

Past the snorkeler who comes up gasping for air in the agitated
   water—

Beak, body, wings spelling out proudly U-O-M—as Dante saw it
   written—MAN in his own language—unmistakably and
   violently on the air,

While the children stare from their boat as from a Russian sleigh,
   the darkening sand blown before them like snow,

The sun, askew, a blob of red quickly cut from Christmas paper,
   the prow of the boat dividing nothing but the oncoming night.

Winter Morning

All night the wind swept over the house
And through our dream
Swirling the snow up through the pines,
Ruffling the white, ice-capped clapboards,
Rattling the windows,
Rustling around and below our bed
So that we rode
Over wild water
In a white ship breasting the waves.
We rode through the night
On green, marbled
Water, and, half-waking, watched
The white, eroded peaks of icebergs
Sail past our windows;
Rode out the night in that north country,
And awoke, the house buried in snow,
Perched on a
Chill promontory, a
Giant's tooth
In the mouth of the cold valley,
Its white tongue looped frozen around us,
The trunks of tall birches
Revealing the rib cage of a whale
Stranded by a still stream;
And saw, through the motionless baleen of their branches,
As if through time,
Light that shone
On a landscape of ivory,
A harbor of bone.

On the Edge

For Gregory on his twenty-first birthday

I

On autumn days when the sky behind
The Vermont mountain opened into a giant gray-blue
Clamshell over us, and birches
By the disjointed skeleton of an old wall
Rose like the thin white spotted legs
Of dangling puppets
We went out to gather mushrooms.
You walked beside me bird-quick, springing
Over wet leaves past the delicate deadly
Amanitas so new and orange-flushed
They seemed to breathe. You crept by them under
A heavy pine branch edged with mist
To pick the ruddy nub of the boletus—
Reaching where I could not reach—
And you were my own arm extending into time,
Bringing reality close up,
Giving color and dimension to the day.

II

On the edge of manhood I found you in an Austrian hotel,
Strong and tall, your black eyes commanding the scene:
You had come down from that higher mountain where
In thin transparent air
Your senses played you false
And the couple on the ledge a mile away
Seemed near enough to touch, the cowbell
On the distant mountain rang next to your ear,
Crisp in the Alpine stillness.

III

There your gaze was true, and you reached
Out to steady me,
Who had tried with you to find
The brother and the son who had lost his way,
Fleeing through hemlock-shaded hollows . . .
And you steadied me that day
Beside a chasm I had barely crossed
Where in a darkening wood below
Pointed fir trees ringed the evening light
And a few stars rose in a clear line
To guide a young man lost.

Elegy for a Young Actor

In a gray New England college town
he was handsome and young
and he played the world for all it was worth,
investing each attempted role
with a spendthrift soul.

Poor in the classroom, poor on the boards,
with a voice that seldom could persuade,
but he won us all when he took the lead
in *The Man with the Flower in His Mouth.*
How his black eyes danced;
how he moved with grace
in light as it peeled the fuzz from his cheek
for one whole week!
How we clapped for him then,
for the cut of his clothes,
and the words that rose
from the depth of his youth!

The curtain came down: one summer day
he took the hand of his leading lady,
a tough little blonde;
together they bowed and moved away.

Five years went by, and then he was back,
his life a wreck,
the tough blonde wife holed up in Back Bay
with the director of another play,
and his parents had long since written him off.

The brilliant lighting now had died,
a curtain had gone down inside.
He strode each day to the liquor store,
his face like the paper bag he bore,
wattled and brown,
to his dim little flat on the edge of town.

And then one morning in less than a year
when he did not appear,
no notices went up,
no flowers arrived,
to mark the end of a failed career.

Lord, I know that the worst
is yet to come, but still I mourn
those who are doomed, cursed
from the start,
who can play but one part,
whose every conscious hour is bleak,
the alcoholic, the addict, and the freak,
the actor who makes it for one week.
I mourn their spooned-out lives, their hobbled youth.
And now while a light snow settles like oblivion
on the graveyard of a gray New England town,
I kneel to place,
in memory, one single-petaled, pink, wild rose
in that young actor's mouth.

Fishing for Albacore

I

Past oil derricks, gray docks, intricate layout of oil pipes, search-
lights wheeling overhead, oil rigs working in darkness with
the motion of praying mantises,

Through gray streets, at 10:00 P.M., down to Pierpont Landing,
Long Beach, where, in the window of a shop offering every
type of fishing gear,

Are displayed fish carved from driftwood by the natives of Bali,
each representing in true colors and exact dimensions a fish
found on their reefs,

Colors derived from bark and root (each fish, when completed, is
bartered for rice; no money is involved);

Then to the Pier, where sixty anglers wait, a bobbing bamboo
wood, to board the *Liberty*, eighty-five feet long, twenty-
three-foot beam, twin diesels, twin stacks painted red, white,
and blue;

And the bamboo surges forward, rustling as in a slow wind, up
the gangplank.

We sail at eleven; stand the poles against the bulkheads, and line
up for rotation tags, my ten-year-old son and I—

Far from those mountains, where, in clear, shallow streams, slim,
speckled trout flicker through massive shadows—

Sail out into San Pedro Bay—Long Beach, San Pedro, Wilmington,
   and below, Huntington Beach and Newport Beach,

Spreading behind us their red, green, and yellow fan of light, while
   one pale blue searchlight, directed from the city's center,
   draws customers to a used car lot;

On until we pull alongside a boat to pick up our live bait, thousands
   of anchovies, handed from a wide brown net, in small dipnets
   on long aluminum poles,

Anchovy-colored, manipulated deftly like giant darning needles,
   anchovies threaded through the nets, dropping into the tanks;

On past the lighthouse, out through the breakwater, where,
   behind us, lit-up oil rigs perched in oily water are grotesque
   festive birds.

Passengers secure their gear; we seek out our bunks below while
   the boat plows ahead into black San Pedro Channel.

We toss for an hour, rough blankets up to our chins, then my son
   wakes me, needing air,

And we climb back on deck, proceed to the bow, where water is
   played out like the scalloped inside of a shell;

Phosphorescence breaks, has broken, into glowing bits of foam
   and then the foam bursts into sprays of flying fish drawn to
   the light;

Our wake swerves into a thousand foaming wings; and then,
   where the waves rise and fall, two waves break, and then two
   more, greener than green,

Not waves but porpoises, darting in and out; the high prow rides
   as if harnessed by dolphins, and my son's head on my shoulder,
   we fly through the night.

II

Below again. 5:00 A.M.; the engines pause, and groggy, back up:
far off to starboard, an island rides in the water, a carrier;

We sit in the galley and wait, or weave along the decks, following
the flying fish, until dawn, and gray water breaks against
gray sky.

8:00 A.M. We stop; rag lures sweep astern; the crew stands aft,
chumming, tossing dipnets of anchovies into the sea to lure
the albacore—if there are albacore—alongside.

And I picture that fish, dark blue above, shading into smoky silver
below, built for great speed, all its fins fitted and grooved, so
that streamlined, steel-blue,

It makes its way in less than a year between Mexico and Japan; and
its spawning grounds are unknown, although one was found
once with ripening ovaries in the late summer off Hawaii,—

The long-winged tuna, *Thunnus alalunga,* esteemed for its white
flesh, weighing up to forty pounds and a real fighter, taking a
trolled lure at eight to ten miles an hour,

That fish the Arabs named *al bukr,* "young camel," of the sea,
watching it weave, blue-humped, with long pectoral fins,
through warm water.

A strike astern; one of the crewmen reels in, and it *is* an albacore;
all sixty poles go over the side, and the deck palpitates with
poles, lines bobbing, weaving, thread tangling;

The waves boil with albacore: fat white bellies, long fins sweeping
up and down in green water and through the school race the
sharks, bloodhounds, blue-green, and the next albacore comes
in, a great chunk chewed from its gut.

The captain fires a shot through the poles to kill the scavenger
while the bloody fish flops its bloated half-belly on the deck
with a hollow gourdlike drumming, and blood runs between
our feet;

Still the poles bend and the fish come in; albacore swoop down,
away, lines play out;

The cry, "Color!" from every side; deckhands rush up with gaffs,
white gasping bodies are hoisted on deck, lines tangle;

Blood on deck, blood in the scuppers, blood and color—"Color!"—
and a fat Japanese boy slips in blood, a fat-bellied fish throb-
bing at his feet;

And through the bamboo forest the sun beats, the sea boils,
tempers break with breaking lines; gulls sweep over the
bloody blue-green, churning cauldron of the sea.

III

After an hour we rotate positions, moving up toward the bow
along the boat's striped divisions.

My son gets a strike; I follow him forward, the pole seeming to
grow from his body, and past the other poles I follow his
tense face

As he dips with the weight of the fish, bobbing, a bright-painted
Russian doll, and I bend to help him steady the pole

And slowly he winds in his prize, boat throbbing, wild water
thrashing

Boat heaves, pole heaves, blood on water, blood on deck, on
clothes, and steady, slowly, in . . .

WHAT TRAIN WILL COME? 208

And there he is—"Color!"—right at the prow where the porpoises
had guided us through the night

And the deckhand with his gaff hoists an albacore more than
half the size of my son, thrashing and throbbing, its dark eye
gazing up and out like a button unthreaded and cut.

IV

Hours pass: fish piling up, sun beating down, blood flowing; the
school of albacore somewhere behind us,

The anglers, winded now, sprawling, the *Liberty* skims along,
giving form to a formless ocean.

Off to port, sudden activity—not albacore, but waterspouts, a
pod of whales . . .

I think of those young Leviathan amours, that harem and its lord
in their indolent rambling, and there somewhere among
them, tail to head, all ready for the final spring, the unborn
whale lying bent like a Tartar's bow . . .

Silence . . . diesel-smell, fish-smell, salt-smell, slip-slap of waves,
the afternoon sun drawing into its wrinkled round all the blood
of the waves.

We speed back to harbor: the boat become a factory, crewmen aft
cleaning fish, blood blowing, hoses running . . .

Throbbing of engines, gulls following, sun riding, winking low,
ribbons of light trailing the horizon,

Waves changing, gray, blue-green, orange, gray, and then the
whole surface weighted, leaden,

Until night comes down, and a semicircle of light dances before us,
    and we whip through the channel, past the lighthouse, a squat
    owl in black water,

Back to the Pier, the blue searchlight spanning the sky, oil rigs
    pumping in the dark, cold light sweeping the *Liberty* as she eases
    in;

And then, plumped down on the pier, in sacks, one hundred
    twenty albacore, whose steel-blue bodies will no longer flash
    on that mysterious migration,

Through that boiling ocean, past whales coupling in foaming
    water, resting mid-earth in the green wavering circle of their
    families,

And we come down to the dock, in hot light, past skeletal poles,
    raw laughter, lights flashing—

Come there to my mother who waits proudly to greet us; and then
    one bright, final flash against the gray (her camera), and there, in
    a circle of light,

As on some permanent atoll, I see my son, smiling, holding his
    fish, reflected, blue and silver, in my mother's eyes.

Three Songs

I. Words by the Water

Beneath the dimming gardens of the sky
That ship, my heart, now rides its anchor chain;
A room is harbor when the world's awry
And life's direction anything but plain.
Still is the wind, and softer still the rain.
Sleep in my arms, my love. O sleep, my love.

Time hangs suspended: with its floating farms,
Its peacock-green and terraced atmosphere,
Now sleep awaits us, love. Lie in my arms;
It is not death but distance that I fear,
Dark is the day, and dangerous the year.
Sleep in my arms, my love. O sleep, my love.

II. Song for a Country Wedding

For Deborah and Marc

We have come in the winter
To this warm country room,
The family and friends
Of the bride and the groom,
To bring them our blessing,
To share in their joy,
And to hope that years passing
The best measures employ
  To protect their small clearing,
  And their love be enduring.

May the hawk that flies over
These thick-wooded hills,
Where through tangled ground cover
With its cushion of quills
The plump porcupine ambles
And the deer come to browse
While through birches and brambles
Clear cold water flows,
   Protect their small clearing,
   And their love be enduring.

May the green leaves returning
To rock maples in spring
Catch fire, and, still burning,
Their flaming coat fling
On the lovers when sleeping
To contain the first chill
Of crisp autumn weather
With log-fires that will
   Protect their small clearing,
   And their love be enduring.

May the air that grows colder
Where the glacier has left
Its erratic boulder
Mountain water has cleft,
And the snow then descending
No less clear than their love
Be a white quilt depending
From sheer whiteness above
   To protect their small clearing,
   And their love be enduring.

III. Mourning Song

Comb the haunted, howling seas,
Count the countless railroad ties,
Nail the rivers to the trees:
  The dead have haddocks' eyes.

Void the cranny, scour the plain,
Scale the peak where no winds rise,
Thread the needles of the rain:
  The dead have haddocks' eyes.

Circle skyward, catch your breath,
Net the bird that blinded flies,
Touch the whirling hem of Death:
  The dead have haddocks' eyes.

Close the silken, quilted lid—
The coffin where your father lies,—
Then stare the dark down as he did:
  The dead have haddocks' eyes.

Then stare the dark down: watch the foam
Of swirling breakers fall and rise
To heave the wild-eyed haddock home:
  The dead have haddocks' eyes.

What Train Will Come?

What train will come to bear me back across so wide a town?

—found scrawled in a subway station

For Jack and Marty Hall

Snowdrifts melt in the streets, pockmarked at the curb
    as by newsprint, and the wind whips up the snow; the air tastes
    of black foam;

The world becomes a wet newspaper into whose blown pages now
    I step, snow mounting all around,

Smudged white walls where howling newsprint peels, tooth-white
    crevasses on which graffiti dance.

The wet dark rushes up as I descend where the black turnstile
    rests, an upended propeller,

And the steps at the edge of the platform echo as if from
    another deserted platform toward another on and on

Like the tapping of miners through the dark; and my heel clicks
    in the cold on a toothless silver comb . . .

What train will come?

Wet clings to my body; gray ash sifts down upon the track
   unwinding ahead, and I can hear far off—or is it far off in the
   mind?—the clang of car on car,

The human chain, the haunted sound; and before me a broken
   mirror swings in the void at the track's edge

And through it cracks spread from a dark center—veins
   like roots tunneling through the ground—

And my step clicks on cement, and whichever way I move—from
   whichever way the train will come—the way is down . . .

While wheels—remembered wheels—turn dizzily before me
   with the broken glass

And in the glass a face that in the silence spreads and turns;
   and in my chest a heartbeat like a distant drum . . .

                    What train will come?

Glass glints; shoe creaks . . . A small child, I walked after
   a tornado in the city, holding my mother's hand,

The sky open again above us like a wound drained of blood, the
   pale edges folded in upon a pink center;

I strolled beside her, and she seemed to spin off from me in
   her dress of voile, her cartwheel hat;

And I gazed out on tilted and shattered telephone poles, their
   wires trailing over sidewalks like black spaghetti;

An acrid taste of burning bread hovered in the air; the most
   intimate parts of buildings had been ripped off, and here
   a bed dangled down

And there was the smell of buried flesh; and I was sick and
  wanted to hide my face and run to some green spot, gaze up
  at a proper sun-lit dome . . .

                        What train will come?

O violent earth: I think of the morning Darwin saw you,
  "the very emblem of all that is solid," a world

That had moved overnight beneath his feet "like a crust over
  a fluid," and when he sailed into Talcahuano Bay

All was strangely still: after the battering waves, water black and
  boiling where the seabed had seemed to crack open;

The shore was strewn with debris, ships keeling over on a
  plain of mud and soggy seaweed,

Burst cotton bales, dead animals, uprooted trees, housetops
  lay tossed about and huge rocks covered the beaches;

And there had been little warning: the first shocks, and then
  the curious twisting movement, making the ground open and
  then close again—as on a tomb . . .

                        What train will come?

But now we do not wait: we rip the earth apart ourselves,
  bulldoze the dead before us,

Make a desert of our blue earth, and explore the desert moon,
  bringing

Her rocks to add to those we pile upon our dead, while in an
  empty landscape of slag heaps

And smoking lagoons the black poor gather under a low sky, and
trapped light hovers like false dawn;

The assassin's bullet is answered by a quiet voice: "Put
your banners down; go quietly home . . ."

And another bullet answers; and still the banners rage and
blaze and burn: Which way is back? Which way is home?

What train will come?

Violence breeds violence until the chain binds and slashes
over burned-over ground

And the distant war is brought closer, diminished on the TV
screen: men kill men, and all three inches tall . . .

In a small skirmish—"little activity, two or three dead,
nothing extraordinary,"

In a country that is soft and wet and hot; now under whirling
chopper blades the grass huts blaze

And the little moon-faced people are lined up for a roll of
color film—men, women, children—and shot down

And with cadaver obedience heaped by rice paddy and rubble—
all to be neatly held one day upon a screen within a frame
of chrome . . .

What train will come?

Three inches tall (in memory) I wander up and down . . . Ah,
once I loved a stone, the shape of water winding through

Wild rose, sweet-william, Indian paintbrush, and in the woods
   a woman (was it my mother?) walking in yellow lace

Through violet shadows, nodding and talking . . . And I left her
   there by the stream . . . and then that night found her again

Locked in a little room at the top of the stairs, moaning and
   calling as if from underground,

And the club that had beaten her rested like some heraldic
   emblem beside the door where the drunken man had placed it;

And I knelt down, staring into my own vomit, helpless, dazed,
   and dumb . . .

               What train will come?

O dreadful night! . . . What train will come? . . . What tree is
   that? . . . a sycamore—the mottled bark stripped bare,

Desolate in winter light against the track, and I continue
   on to the mud-flats

By the roaring river where garbage, chicken coops, and houses
   rush by me on mud-crested waves,

And at my feet are dead fish—catfish, gars—and there in a
   little inlet

Come on a deserted camp, the tin can in which the hoboes brewed
   their coffee stained bitter black

As the cinders sweeping ahead under a milkweed-colored sky
   along a darkening track

And gaze into a slough's green stagnant foam,
and know that the way out is never back,

but down,

down . . .

What train will come

to bear me back

across so wide a town?

THE TRAVELER'S TREE

(1980)

At Delphi

For Allen Tate on his seventy-fifth birthday

I

This morning on the edge of Parnassus we watched the old women
    at Arakhova, where the houses

Rise in terraces on the mountain spur, black kerchiefs knotted
    at their throats,

Holding spools of cotton in their crooked hands like the unformed
    substance of life

Itself, drawing the thread out from below, whipping it in blue
    light through agile fingers;

That thread has followed us throughout the day at Delphi among
    the ruins,

Cicadas stitching the dry air, which Plutarch found "close and
    compact

With a tenseness caused by reflection of the mountains and their
    resistance,

But at the same time fine and biting . . . as fine and close
    as silk,"

Has followed us past temple, treasury, theatre, and stadium to the
    edge of that spring

Separating with its white tongue the twin Phaeriades, the Shining
    Rocks,

Where in niches above green water black and white butterflies,
    their wings

Patterned like ancient pottery, hovered in the heat; has followed
    us to that oval

Spindle-plaited stone that marked the place where those two
    eagles released

By Zeus—one from the east and one from the west—once met, to
    that

Omphalos, cut and tied by the legendary Earth-mother, to the navel
    of the world.

II

Far from this earth center, guarded by the python coiling from its
    seismic chasm,

To the hot dry Kentucky of your youth, where "long shadows of
    grapevine wriggle and run over the green swirl,"

Far from the tulip tree and the creek road winding under the
    quicksilver sky,

Where the drowsing copperhead kept watch beside the water "that
    bells and bickers

All night long," far from that shaded path beside the swimming
    hole, where you saw

The black man's body fallen from the tree, and saw it dragged
    unclaimed

Into the town, far from that clear spring of love that broke through multiple

Layers of memory to recreate that scene and find that the central evil of this earth

May be redeemed in art, as here within a frame of sculpted palmette and lotus

Mythic scenes depict a continuing triumph against barbarian invaders; I think of you

And of your victory now while cicadas echo through the valley, and the twin reflecting rocks

Reflect the pink and amber light, down the darkening precipice as far as the mirroring

Sea of Corinth, and the olive trees below us here take on the verdigris of a great

Bronze shield deposited on the stone-ribbed slope in an ancient battle between giants.

III

The thread of light unwinds around the cypresses like blue-black spools,

Along the gold-green edges of pine needles; and bats sweep forth as if released

On thread, skimming, dipping, knitting together the last frayed patches

Of light. Parnassus draws in upon itself, and in the pit-stillness now I hear

A voice asking: "Who among you doubts whether thunder sends
forth a voice?"

And now hear thunder breaking like clear water from the rocks,
and hear

The oracle speak again from out the centuries, its message clear
and understood:

"What can survive this light if it is not language?" and hear as
in your poem

Hoofbeats resounding on a dim and dusty road; and now the
cicadas cease;

The night draws fully in, thread over fine, thin fingers at the
center of the earth.

Venice in the Fog

For Sonja, con amore

I

Fog in mid-December has descended on Venice; and the city wraps
   itself around itself

Like the sea horses we have seen in the aquarium, tails linked,
   twisting, turning,

Rising gently to the green surface of the water; the water of
   Venice, a mirror,

Is held up on all sides so that the bridge reflected rises and
   drifts toward us, a twisted turret,

And the city, lighter than goose down, is about to float through
   the air—

Or rest, a hulk, a battleship stranded, gray on gray sand, green
   barnacles encrusting

Its gray guns; the silver of the mirror is rubbed away so that
   one looks not into, but through, the glass,

And moves in a carnival, where black masks wander up and down,
   and the people wearing them

Are nowhere to be seen—they're lost in fog—and the buildings
   come at you through holes in the masks;

Bodies—ghosts' bodies—brush by you in the mist; the Bridge
of Sighs is an eyelid

Lifted on a gray eyeball; and behind it a red boat light slowly
streaks with blood.

II

St. Mark's bursts at us through fog, the mottled, humped face of
a bright tropical fish;

The Doge's Palace beside it rests on the intaglio of its pillars,
a stranded fish skeleton.

The *acqua alta* has subsided; in dim pools in the square the
pigeons huddle in the cold,

Flying apart of a sudden like a fringe of wool, purple threads
at their throats,

And one, frayed and battered, limps off toward the ruby glow of a
jeweled shop,

And, nuzzling its head against a column, falls over dead, its
mauve feathers the wet wisps of an old broom.

Fragments of buildings—architraves, cornices, pediments—fly
through the night

And here at our feet, a group of gondolas tied together sit, squat,
a row of black, muzzled dogs.

The lighted shops are so many bright boxes spilling out into the
night—gold, glass beads

Falling beside the water like multiple chains from the throats of
Venetian women.

Now in La Fenice—the fog behind us—we are inside the golden
   box, and below us women in Minoan dress

Sing out their lives, and fall spent on amber rocks . . . And now pink
   lobster, eel,

Layers of encrusted crayfish swim toward us through the gray
   light where streetlights drift,

The blue-pink pods of the medusa . . . And our forks come down
   upon the plate,

Cutting through the fog; we begin to bite into Venice, tasting
   its hidden, sea-green sweetness.

III

Three days and the fog gives no sign of lifting (after three days
   of fog it rains, they tell us) . . .

Cats go masked; white-veiled, bulging flower shops float off,
   barges bearing the remnants

Of bridal festivities . . . I touch their perfume as they move
   away; and from here in the room gaze down

On the bridge below and the shops beside it held in marbled water,
   veins of mist cutting

Through it while my pen on the page cuts through veined layers of
   consciousness . . .

Domes, arched windows rising toward me are bushes bent down
   with snow and ice; and the saints from their niches

Fly out like birds, all saying: Life is neither nightmare nor dream
   but dream and reality converging;

Heaven, as Blake knew, can be met with anywhere, and what
    cannot be seen must be imagined and seen more clearly . . .

Here seven years ago I walked at night through the fog, my steps
    echoing behind me;

My past life rose up unmasked before me; and even then I could
    see your face—a face I had not yet seen—

Swim toward me—a bright fine-boned face parting the spray
    before it, the figurehead of a ship . . .

And I gaze down now into the fog, and hear behind me—echoing
    up through my life—

Your steps on the stair; you come in, cold from your walk, and
    toss your purple cape on the bed, its fur wet from the fog;

Your hair falls red about your throat; you turn from the gold room
    and run the water in the bath,

Steam rising from it like fog; and below me footsteps echo on the
    pavement; bell buoys clang in the distance . . .

You step from your warm bath and lie down beside me; my hand
    moves over the nipples of your breast,

Down over the firm belly and rests on your thigh; as the mirror
    breaks in a thousand pieces,

The room is all pomegranate and gold; the fog clears—parting
    as if for the marriage of Venice with the sea—

And all that could not be seen is seen, all that was imagined, is, all
    that was lost, found.

Journey to the Dead Sea

*Fishermen will stand beside the sea; from En-gedi to En-eglaim it will be
a place for the spreading of nets; its fish will be of very many kinds, like
the fish of the Great Sea. . . . And on the banks, on both sides of the river,
there will grow all kinds of trees for food. Their leaves will not wither nor
their fruit fail, but they will bear fresh fruit every month, because the water
for them flows from the sanctuary. Their fruit will be for food and their
leaves for healing.*

—Ezekiel 47:10–12

For Robert Penn Warren

I

On the outskirts of Tel Aviv a dromedary is chained in a vacant lot
near a junkyard,

And soon the orange groves begin: on the right, a railroad to the
Gaza strip,

A highway to bring potash to Ashdod; on the left, the mountains
of Judah.

Our bus driver maneuvers, stares ahead; in the green frog-goggles
of our guide pass

Rows of eucalyptus, pecan plantations; he drones on from under
his baseball cap:

"And so in 1946 the Jews built eleven villages overnight, for by
Turkish law

Dwelling was occupation, and the British must respect what
was done . . ."

His accent thick as German pickles, his tongue heavy on each
syllable, he squats

Before us, cap twisted to one side, as if ready to shuffle into some
burlesque routine,

His jokes as old as time, as alive as the weather, survivor of Buchen-
wald, green-checked and goggled.

"Each country has its problem. We have our problem. Who is a
Jew? What is a Jew? . . .

"In Haifa," he booms, "the cinemas are closing; they're turning into
wedding halls . . ."

And his voice reaches back over the shaded green seats, coming
not from the loudspeaker

But rising, dark life-force, from time itself. Life, it seems to say,
is there to be enjoyed;

And I am that fool in the legend who guides you on all your
journeys back

Into yourself, who takes his own long journey back to his village,
and looks up

At his native sky, saying, I have traveled far, but to this final place
I come

Where the sky is as clear as it was in my own village; this is my
place; here I am home.

II

And here the descent begins: after dusty Beersheba with its
   hibiscus and pepper trees,

Where, in the dark hotel interior, pink roses rest frozen in wax,
   and olives have the cold flavor of underground

Wells, Beersheba, where early each morning the Bedouins come to
   bargain

For dromedaries; after Dimonah, in Hebrew "wasting," where the
   sewage water

Is used and reused; after a textile factory, a domed atomic reactor
   perched

Like a mosque in the distance, the desert begins, breaks off in
   pieces—

The hills break off—and there three gasoline drums, rusting
   below us,

Are tucked between boulders; and down the slope a piece of flint
   flicking the heat,

A gazelle. We wind down past the carcass of a junked car robin's-
   egg blue,

And the heat wavers, rests in folds of rock; wind down through
   earth's deepest depression,

Down through the cut—the *ghor*—there to a curve, where the bus
   draws up

Beside a rust-red overturned truck where tourists are eating
   watermelon, its wet red flesh

Blood dripping among boulders, its black seed scattered around
them like dim

Figures of Bedouins disappearing in the heat; and we gaze out
through shimmering heat waves,

White salt smoke pouring upward in newly hatched green insect
stripes—

Where does land stop and sea begin?—gaze out through heat
more visible

Than a mirage upon that fabled Salt Sea, *Yam Ha-Melach,* stretching
north and south,

Sea of Lot, *Bahr Lut,* the Eastern Sea, Sea of Overwhelming, Sea
of the Plain,

Sea of the Arabah, Dead Sea, *Lacus Asphaltites,* Lake of Bitumin,
ten miles across,

Forty-six miles long, the stagnant green surface lying thirteen
hundred feet below the Mediterranean,

And thirteen hundred feet deep—gaze out on the thick, gassy,
bitter waters

In which no fish live, over which no birds fly; where the ancient
traveler saw

No plants rising in the poisonous air along the shore but forests
of legendary pine

In its green depth, and, wavering among them, the burnt, scarred,
toppled towers of the Cities of the Plain.

III

No birds, no fish; but the valley is a fish skeleton, the striated
  rib cage

Of a whale, which we enter, skirting green decaying flesh flaking
  off through the air—

Fresh water rising in vapor along the blazing rocks lining wind-
  worn wadies—

The white marl of *Al Lisan,* the tongue, dividing the green surface—
  the mucus-like basins

Of the bromide factories, where green water is made greener to
  hasten evaporation—

On through hallucinatory green—to Mount Sodom, where a
  huge squat rock figure—

Wind-ruffled and worn, looking like Queen Victoria surveying
  her dead domain—Mrs. Lot, our guide tells us,

Who, not obeying her master, has become a salt pillar; and then
  Masada, cut off by two wadies,

Perched where blue-white clouds form over the valley—a final
  refuge

After the fall of Jerusalem, where nine hundred and sixty-seven
  Jews chose suicide rather than surrender—

Their ghosts for centuries circling the yellow outcroppings on the
  plateau of Judea,

Where, as at Auschwitz, "a clear sky spreads over the shaven
  skulls," and, below, at Kallia

We enter the sea itself, six times saltier than any ocean: the bus, in
   a flood-lit nightmare,

Discharges its odd passengers on the hot shore: the mouse-man
   from Detroit, the eaglet sculptress from California,

A red bandanna knotted round her head, the prim straw-hatted
   duck from Brooklyn, the dodo, the jay—

All bobbing in grease-thick water up to our armpits below tooth-
   pick telephone poles

Receding in the distance—under the green-goggled eyes of our
   guide—

Afloat in this interior ocean salt-scaled, tasting and smelling of
   salt—

The plain of Moab drifting above us like the back of a bloated
   camel at a dried-up waterhole—

Released in an ever-renewed pool of tears at the bottom of the
   world.

IV

In the Bedouin's tent as if high on a camel's hump, tent poles
   slanting and swaying,

We rest in the desert heat: ashes in the center brew coffee while
   earth

Sways with the tent's panels: in memory the afternoon sways,
   sinks and rises—

Draws up that level sunken sea with its twisted salt-coated rocks,
   that glaucous pit

Where death itself appeared to reject us, that sulphurous sea in
    the deep-faulted desert;

And in the shifting fire, its coals like fruits "that tempt the eye,
    but turn to ashes on the lips"—

In the gathering dust of the apples of Sodom—we watch, remem-
    bering, yellow sand move

And from the sand gazelles that clatter down the cliffside; and
    there from some faulted point

Deep in the earth on that inner ear that bears all memory of sound
    imprinted in fossil now breaks

A sudden rush of clear water, falling as from Himalayan heights,
    sweet water cutting through bitter rock

To a desert of thorn trees, to the briars and hollow apples there
    at the edge

Of the Salt Sea, into a brake of rushes and reeds, the oasis of
    En-gedi,

David's green refuge, a place of caverns and strongholds, where
    the soul knows

That in gardens of cucumber and melon it will taste water that
    has worked its hidden

Way through deepest desert, and, touching the planet's most
    poisoned spot,

Falls on a clear pool, tilting with stars, encircled with smooth
    rocks and cress,

On that healing place this side of death that can be reached only
    through knowledge and pain.

The Traveler's Tree

Its common name derives from its having hollow bases to its leaf stalks from which it is said that travelers obtained drinking water. The traveler's tree has a palmlike trunk up to 30 feet in height and immense long-stemmed, paddle-shaped leaves arranged in two ranks spread in one plane like a gigantic fan. Although the leaves do not naturally divide, they are usually more or less shredded by wind action.

—Thomas H. Everett, *Living Trees of the World*

I

On a day like this so clear that your eye
can carry you over the beckoning curve of the horizon
you will be lifted slowly on wings that seem
to touch the end of time—
lifted in memory or dream—
and the golden cubes of buildings will settle on green banks
or tumble into the bronze river,
monumental amber pieces from the broken necklace of a giantess:
on such a day in the late afternoon you will begin your journey.

You will travel in a series of perfect ever-present moments,
moments just past that you can never retrieve
and yet will hold forever: you will leave
behind you constant flashing scenes—
sunlight dappling clear spring water
until grasses growing in green depths
surround you of a sudden like a fringe of willows
on a sandbank in midsummer—
and all that had been wavering within is there without.

The world will open then before you; you will move over a snow-swirled
landscape, carried along as palpably as snow
that obliterates black rock
and weighs down thick pine branches—
borne along still fjords until you reach a point
where ice breaks off, and you rest on blue water,
and prisms of ice drift past you,
melting with the changing seasons into a quiet sea.

And now you cross that sea: the prow of your ship
cuts through blue-black water with a sound like the tearing of silk,
and phosphor rides in your wake
to the edge of the stars: the great cross
hangs above you on the wrinkled cassock of the south;
and chains of dolphins guide you between shaggy, humpbacked islands.

To the left, a light cascades across the sky,
pulsing pink, then red, and deeper red,
the rambling petals of a giant rose gone wild,
flung in profusion down the mountainside:
a volcano that erupts, its rumble muffled by the wind,
its shadow sifting down dustlike on your face and on the waves
until the night explodes in pulsing pink and the ship
in the sea's dark troughs rides, a veering worm,
into the heartbeat of the world become a rose.

II

Through a white coral passage that appears
no wider than your body's width,
you move into a final harbor, an atoll's closed lagoon,
staring into space, the earth's eyeball,
and its clear coral depth contains, the frozen garlands
of former travelers, a lifetime's thoughts,
around which circle striped and spotted fish.
A thousand sea birds, frigates, terns,
weaving, whirling, conduct you to the shore
and to a fronded, mottled path—

through lianas enveloping a rich, decaying vegetation—
to a clearing, where, on a green mound,
little more than a swelling of the ground,
its central opening, a wide, dark mouth rising to catch the wind,
rests the low-lying house.

III

There shoulder-high, the leaves long-stemmed
and paddle-shaped, arranged in two ranks spread
in one plane,
into a wind-shredded, green, gigantic fan—
the turkey headdress of some Cherokee chieftain—
rises the traveler's tree
in white hot light,
trunk resting on the dwarf, ignorant earth,
the many arms of Siva fringed in fire—
life entire—
creator and destroyer, magnificent wild dancer,
whom even the gods lean down to see,
the mystic tree, the traveler's tree.

Break off a branch, a leaf stalk: from its hollow base
drink, as from some deep well of air,
its water, long-collected, cold and clear.
And breaking off that branch, you will break off your dream
and be again a boy in a small boat
drinking from a paddle
the transparent water of a mountain stream.

Then cross the threshold and enter the dark house.
You will be welcome. I will be waiting. I will be there.

JOURNEY
TO THE INTERIOR
(1980–1989)

After the Hurricane

After the hurricane on the island of St. Croix,
apparently the bees,
finding the flowers everywhere stripped and shredded,
turned to people, seeking on the human body
the nectar needed for survival.

And I have thought for days now of that green island—
of the trees bent and bare,
twisted like old coat-hangers,
the clothing they had borne,
along with ripped and gutted houses,
scattered over the soggy ground . . .

and have heard at my back
the constant humming of those circling bees,
and in huge frothing clouds have smelled the perfume
of remembered cascading blossoms,

and seen far off great waves break
on the earth's rim as on a giant's thigh . . .
and felt the foam uncurl along a coral reef
as over a necklace of skulls.

A Sculptor, Welding

Life meanders, jumps backwards and forwards,
draws netted patterns like those on the musk melon.
It seems the most formless of things.

—Ford Madox Ford

Life meanders, jumps backwards and forwards . . .
And brings you to a rust-walled, oil-splotched garage
in Brooklyn, where this morning, in helmet, goggles, and gloves,
cap shielding hair from bumblebees of fire,
past hammers, hacksaws, and pliers stowed in neat lines,
you gaze for a long while—spaceman into space—
("It is not hard to work," Brancusi said, "it is hard to *begin* to work")
on broken machine parts, gears, slats, chains, boiler-heads,
automobile bumpers, axle splines,
salvaged from junkyards and dumps,
the skeletal framework of an entire
industrial empire. . . .

And you begin: hoist slabs of steel—
each lifelike pursuing its own path, one, a windmill spinning,
another, revolving midair in your mind, a paddlewheel,
another, a gangplank down to a sandbar
where willows reach to the water's edge,
and stranded alone there now, you dredge
up from the mud-thick depth of that multilayered stream—
life's netted patterns drawn into another net—
disc-sanded to reflect a waiting sky—
the lost configuration of a dream.

And lifted now on wild, imagined wind, the steel slabs
lose all weight, sweep back with the elegance of drapery,
and fly like feathers in a storm
to their new destination:
caught in the hurricane-eye, the pencil point
of your flame's white cone
(as if in your hands you held the netted stars),
you guide the tempered steel and weld it down to rest
in lucid air, in blue and lasting peace,
out of life's formlessness, now form.

On the Death of a Poet's Infant Son
Michael Jasper Gioia, aged four months

Rose, elle a vécu ce que vivent les roses,
L'espace d'un matin.

—Malherbe

Malherbe's daughter lived as roses do
Just long enough to see the morning through;
But Michael was a bud brought fresh to light
Which Death broke off and took into the night.

Litany for a Rainy Night

The distant highway hums: you lie alone,
  Bone-cold your narrow bed and black the air.
Tonight the stones have wept, but stones are stone.
The distant highway hums: you lie alone.
Dead men have also wept, but for bare bone
  What have they with the living left to share?
The distant highway hums: you lie alone,
  Bone-cold your narrow bed and black the air.

Journey to the Interior

He has gone into the forest,
to the wooded mind in wrath;
he will follow out the nettles
and the bindweed path.

He is torn by tangled roots,
he is trapped by mildewed air;
he will feed on alder shoots
and on fungi: in despair

he will pursue each dry creek-bed,
each hot white gully's rough raw stone
till heaven opens overhead
a vast jawbone

and trees around grow toothpick-thin
and a deepening dustcloud swirls about
and every road leads on within
and none leads out.

Gardens

For Stanley Kunitz, poet and gardener,
on his eightieth birthday

"Now that is what I call a garden!" the reluctant Texan tourist
exclaimed to his wife. He gestured from the upper balcony
of Powis Castle, on the border between Wales and England,
toward a wealth of statuary, Italianate balustrades
and stairways, lush perennial borders, formal terraces
(each with its distinctive feature, the first, a line of yews
like a row of giant gnomes' hats hung along the walls)
spilling over with musk roses, wisteria and clematis
to a green park-like basin below
and the cloud-swept Shropshire hills off in the distance.

Your Cape Cod garden is a far more modest affair,
having all that a garden needs,
"plain bricks, wood, water, and plenty of plants,"
as that essential earthman, Henry Mitchell, would declare,
a place the color of earth and air,
that makes you feel, when you step into it,
that you have come out of a desert
and found, as if dreaming,
a Rousseau-like jungle, dripping and steaming,
where passion like the peony may have its province
and simple impatiens flower in the shade,
where daffodils flare back like mules' ears,
a place where one may sit and mull things over,
savoring, from the darkest depths, with your trumpeting vines,
your stiff grass spears,
your billowing trees,

a poet's lines,
reminding us that gardening, like the writing of poetry,
is among the most natural and rewarding—
and yet most mysterious—of human activities.

Wedding Song

For Evita and Gregory

I would have instruments that could express
The captive music of clear mountain streams,
The shafted sunlight and the moon's cold beams,
A keyboard so attuned it could address
The songs recorded by your deepest dreams,
To speak for joy, keep discontent at bay
To wish you well upon your wedding day.

I would have baroque fountains cast in bronze
Where water would enclose with silver veils
Sea creatures half encased in virid scales,
And rising, fall, and rise against green lawns
In crystal iridescent peacock tails
Until each eye is dazzled by the spray
To wish you well upon your wedding day.

I would have pinewoods open to a sky
So spicy clear that you could touch the stars,
Lilacs rain-drenched to smell, and cool sandbars
To lie upon, rare pungent herbs to dry
And, memory compacted, store in jars,
And fireflies in a field of new-mown hay
To wish you well upon your wedding day.

I'd have persimmons picked within a glade
Where pheasant for your table moved among
Gold aromatic grass with berries hung,
Goose liver, pink as baby flesh, inlaid
With truffles that, dissolving, drug the tongue,
With salmon, oysters, wine in sweet array
To wish you well upon your wedding day.

I have only words but words are strong;
For if our senses are a kind of sieve
To filter out the rich life that we live,
Then from such riches words can shape a song
To offer up the joy that I would give
And to you thus the greatest wealth convey
To wish you well upon your wedding day.

Sitting Bull in Serbia

(at Vršac)

A hundred years ago, they say, Buffalo Bill
Brought his Wild West Show—
And, with it, Sitting Bull—
Here to Vršac.
People came to stare at the western warrior,
His weathered face mottled and brown
As a raisin from their vineyards;
And what did he see, the old chief,
When, dark-eyed, he returned their stare?
When the carnival dust settled
And the war whoops died, what did he see
Beyond the hoopla of the ring,
The wild, phony, stampeding horses?
In a twisting thread of smoke
Rising from the square
He saw perhaps the shrouded mountains of his boyhood;
In the embroidered dresses of peasant women,
The flashing pebbles of clear streams;
In the somber, tassled jacket of the men
The outline of a circling eagle's wings.
And far off, above the House of the Two Pistols,
Where Black George, leader of the Serbian revolt,
Had hidden,
High above the Bishop's Palace,
Over the town's brooding tower,
He saw the Earth's Great Spirit
Hover for a moment,
And then, with a shaggy, humpbacked bison,
Plunge down the western sky
Headlong into the night.

The Players

In May 1840, during the Second Seminole War, the players of a traveling Shakespearean troupe left their baggage unattended near St. Augustine, Florida, and a band of Seminoles made off with it into the swamp. The following March at Fort Cummings the Seminole Chief Coacoochee ("The Wild Cat") and his followers appeared to discuss a treaty with General Walker Keith Armistead, Commander of the United States forces. Coacoochee came forward wearing on his brow the ostrich feathers of Hamlet, Prince of Denmark, and his followers were ornamented with the spangles and bright-colored vests that form the basis of the present-day costume of the Seminoles, who withdrew into the Everglades and never surrendered. Hamlet's headgear became the badge of the Seminole Medicine man.

A curtain of green divides—and there they are:
the Wildcat Hamlet, black-caped, plumed, and nodding,
Horatio at one side, and on the other,
in silken turban, an opal at one ear, Othello—
or is he the slave who fled the Georgian whip?—
then Richard, grim and brooding in his royal purple,
together with the Fool, whose cap and bells
capture the faintest breeze like wind-chimes . . .
and slowly they advance toward you, General,
seated before your table in the clearing.

Stiff-pleated, soldiers gape;
a bugle sounds; the drummer taps his drum
as if for the cortege of a fallen comrade.

The curtain divides, but, General, for you
dream and reality converge; and reason slumbers.
Your nightmare surfaces; your enemy has risen from the swamp.

And with the drumbeat, rain that you have heard
these many months upon the barracks roof,
a steady tap-tap-tap-tap, then stopping . . . tap . . . tap . . .
tap . . . and then again tap-tap tap-tap,
as unending as the oratory on the Congress floor
to justify an unjustifiable war, to round up
a few Indians, burn their crops and bribe them
to be herded onto ships at Tampa
and carried westward to a barren dust bowl. . . .
You hear the constant sloshing of your troops
through ever-present water . . .

. . . and lifted to your steady gaze, the swamp's black mirror,
cut by alligator-blade and skeletal palmetto,
swathe of egret feathers, the heron's bony legs,
dainty stag hoof, dank panther paw, the seething saw grass,
the fangs of water moccasins, the smear of glutinous eggs,
a swarm of black flies circling the even blacker water
like a convocation of Jesuits,
croaking frog-chorale that kept you company at midnight,
the fret and freckle of the water round the grass-fringed
   hammock,
the woodpecker's crimson vest, the spider's velvet net,
all the sequins and the spangles of that savage light,
the rich, wild, ranging necklaces of root,
green, unfolding fans, striped scarves, and spotted feathers,
the stately live oak trailing gray Spanish moss
(the shredded rags of Lear upon the heath),
the cypress knees protruding from the water
(the knuckles of your fallen dead
whose ghosts have grappled with the mist),
the purple cape of sunset dragging its ermine edge
across the mangrove thicket,—
all are mirrored here before you, General: your enemy
has come in the nightmare clothing of the swamp.

Tap . . . tap . . . tap . . .
                    Hamlet advances,
holding in one hand a skull—
or is that only a piece of coral from the reef
with all the perforations of the human brain? . . .

You watch it crumble, General, at your feet,
while your euclidian table projects into the waning light,
and the paper beneath your eagle-talon
rests, a white, fallen feather.

—A wild wind rakes your fort, a hurricane
across the tense peninsula . . .
                    and in the silent eye
a voice that cleaves the quiet water:

"There will be no surrender, General. There will be no peace;
only the murderer who waits, only the poetry that kills."

811.54 Smith, William Jay,
SMI   1918-

      Collected poems

     $24.95

DATE			